A KOSHER COOKBOOK

OUR TABLE

TIME-TESTED RECIPES • MEMORABLE MEALS

RENEE MULLER

PHOTOGRAPHY
Daniel Lailah

FOOD AND PROP STYLING
Renee Muller

DESIGN
Miller Creative & Devorah Cohen

COVER DESIGN
RADesign

PUBLISHER
Mesorah Publications, Ltd.

Published by **ARTSCROLL / SHAAR PRESS**
4401 Second Avenue / Brooklyn, NY 11232 / (718) 921-9000 www.artscroll.com

Distributed in Israel by **SIFRIATI / A. GITLER**
Moshav Magshimim / Israel

Distributed in Europe by **LEHMANNS**
Unit E, Viking Business Park, Rolling Mill Road Jarrow, Tyne and Wear, NE32 3DP / England

Distributed in Australia and New Zealand by **GOLDS WORLD OF JUDAICA**
3-13 William Street / Balaclava, Melbourne 3183, Victoria / Australia

Distributed in South Africa by **KOLLEL BOOKSHOP**
Northfield Centre / 17 Northfield Avenue / Glenhazel 2192 Johannesburg, South Africa

ISBN-10: 1-4226-1760-2 / ISBN-13: 978-1-4226-1760-1

Printed in Canada

ACKNOWLEDGMENTS

I take a moment to look back at the last few years, and I am humbled by the amount of good the Almighty has bestowed upon me; providing me with opportunity and the strength to pursue it. **HASHEM** has His ways in getting us to where we belong, slowly but steadily.

This journey began in May 2011, when *Ami Magazine* first welcomed me to their team. My column, "A Tavola," ran for four incredible years. I was able to meet and learn from creative talent in all fields, forging new friendships along the way. Personalities like **LEAH SCHAPIRA** and **VICTORIA DWEK**, believed in me and guided me to where I am today. They directed me to the food styling profession, which I continue to practice to this day. Furthermore, countless phone calls, emails, and hours were spent discussing detail after detail while writing this book. Leah and Victoria have been there for me all along and selflessly shared their time and their experience.

Writing for *Ami* honed my skills as a food writer. I am grateful to **RABBI FRANKFURTER** and **MRS. RECHY FRANKFURTER**, who provided a platform for me to write, create recipes, and connect to my devoted readers.

I thank **MY READERS** for giving me constructive criticism along the way, helping me perfect my product. Your enthusiasm and support always warmed my heart and galvanized my will to keep writing.

I thank the entire ArtScroll/Mesorah team for their professionalism and dedication, but mostly, for making me part of the "family." Thank you, **GEDALIAH ZLOTOWITZ**, for being so kind and accommodating at all times, helping with all the details and smoothing out the unavoidable bumps in the road. **MRS. EISNER**, your expertise on the written word continues to amaze. Thank you for putting so much devotion and care into every little comma. **DEVORAH COHEN**, your talent and skill show throughout the book; there's nothing you can't get done, with style.

Thank you, **DANIEL LAILAH**, our world-class photographer, for going out of your way and caring about each step of the process. Your incredible photography and attenttion to detail are what makes this book so beautiful.

Thank you, **MIRIAM COHEN** and **JENNA GRUNFELD**, my trusted assistants, for bearing with me and helping me get it all done with maximum efficiency while still remembering to have fun.

Thank you, all the women who took the time to test and retest recipes so that perfection is achieved, every time.

Thank you, **GITTY SPITZ**, my loyal sister, who's always there for me, especially when I need it the most.

I owe everything I know to the many women in my life. Those who took time to advise, explain, and demonstrate how things are done. The creative aunt named Zia, the many sisters and sisters-in-law who tasted and critiqued. The grandmothers who cooked without cookbooks, using handfuls for cups and smaller handfuls for tablespoons. Who knew how to fix a recipe by its smell or to season *"biz sekimt tzim taam"* (Yiddish for "until it gets to its flavor"), as **BOBBI LEITCHU** *a"h* would say.

MOMMY, my mother-in-law, taught me how to cook and how to find my way around a new country, giving me advice and tips I use daily. Her most valuable lesson is that cooking with joy and love always results in tastier food.

IMA, my mother, taught me everything I know about using fresh produce and not taking shortcuts. Her patience and diligence are admirable. She taught me how to plan a meal, a Shabbos, a three-day Yom Tov. To think ahead and get to the finish line, unfazed. This is the woman who took us on Friday afternoons to enjoy an espresso at the Piazza. Because Shabbos was ready, and Friday was ours, she filled it with memories of calm and poise.

Last but never least, I thank **MY HUSBAND** and **CHILDREN** (you will get to know them throughout this book as Child A, B, C, D, and E). Thank you for putting up with me while I tested and retested family favorites (until they risked not being so favorite anymore), patiently telling me what needed what and what missed where. You are my best and favorite critics; you are not afraid to be brutally honest or overly excited by my creations. Your constant help in the kitchen is what I value most. And we always have so much fun along the way.

As our architect and family friend Harrison Baldinger wisely said while our house was being built, "No matter what you do, invest primarily in your kitchen. That is where the family gathers, it's the heart of the home."

How right he was.

TABLE OF CONTENTS

INTRODUCTION

A tavola — (Italian) literal translation: at the table.

Usually pronounced "A taaaaaaaavooolaaaaaaaa!" and yelled at an incredibly loud decibel level, preferably while wearing a well-used apron and holding a wooden spoon covered in sauce.

Most commonly used by all Italian *mamme* (my Ima included) as an approach to gather all family members to the table.

A tavola is where we gather. To talk, to socialize, to catch up .... And to eat. Our table is where it all comes together. The people, the food, the *joie de vivre*. Because it is not only about the food; it is about stopping whatever we are doing and carving out some much-needed time to nourish our souls and our bodies in the company of our loved ones.

Our table is where life and food meet.

Italian is a phonetic language. Easy to learn, without many rules to memorize. What you hear is what you write, and vice versa. Yet the word *table*, is a fascinating exception to the rule. A table, in Italian, is *tavolo*, in masculine form. A simple description of what it is: a piece of furniture. Yet, once that same table is set with plates, cups, knives, spoons, and forks, ready for a meal, its name transforms. It becomes *tavola*, in the feminine. The table comes to life. It literally changes its definition. This rings so true to me and is so very Italian.

Growing up in the beautiful city of Lugano, Switzerland, is a big part of who I am today. My view on life, the way I perceive my surroundings, hope to raise my children, and yes, cook and bake, are all reflections of my unique childhood. I grew up with traditional European values, taught to me by my parents and grandparents. We lived in a close knit community where every person was respected and cherished, and every occasion shared and celebrated as one. My neighbors were my cousins, my classmates my family. Some through blood, others through friendship. Sephardic, Ashkenazi, BT, or FFB — it didn't matter. The community was warm, everyone belonged.

We shared our joys and our sorrows. Our ups and our downs. Our recipes and our food.

Even as a little girl, I enjoyed spending time in the kitchen beside my mother and grandmother, watching them cook and talk, always with passion and dedication to the task at hand, no matter how mundane. Already then I knew: I wanted my home to have that same welcoming aroma of freshly homemade meals and that same loving attention to detail. Meals were planned according to what was in season, desserts prepared according to what was being celebrated.

This wonderful feeling is something I carried with me all the way to Lakewood, New Jersey. With a home to call my own, I started experimenting with my brand-new pots and pans, learning the best way one learns anything — through trial and error. And by taking lots of advice. And recipes. From neighbors or friends, a nurturing mother-in-law and a patient sister-in-law. Everyone can teach you something, because, I've learned, everyone has something to teach.

Slowly, my repertoire and style for cooking came together, a cuisine that is *heimish* yet laced with aromas of my youth. Lots of fresh produce, genuine ingredients, and a joy for cooking helped me create recipes that stood the test of time. I cook for my family, and sometimes *with* my family. But it is always *for* them, with them only on my mind.

The joyful expression on my child, who's excited to discover a favorite dish is cooking in the oven, is what makes me strive to continue cooking, day in and day out, no matter the circumstances.

A mother's love is to be used like any other spice. Put it into the food and you will taste the difference.

I welcome you to join our table, our recipes, and the foods that make my family happy. This book is called *Our Table* because that is exactly what it is. Our children's table, our friends' table, and our loved one's table. And now, your table as well.

ICON GUIDE

M || MEAT

D || DAIRY

P || PAREVE

FF || FREEZER FRIENDLY

GF || GLUTEN FREE (NOTATED ONLY IN *BREADS, CAKES & COOKIES* AND *DESSERTS* SECTIONS)

VIDEO GUIDE

Many times, while writing down recipe instructions, I wished I could just invite you all to join me in my kitchen and cook with me. There is only so much one can convey on paper ...

That thought led me to the idea of presenting a variety of videos to show you, in the comfort of your own home, the techniques I use for some of my recipes.

I hope you will find these videos useful, and better yet, enjoyable. Please sit back and relax as I take pleasure in welcoming you into my own kitchen.

The recipes listed on the right have links to videos showing the techniques (and equipment) I use to prepare them. Go to www.artscroll.com/ourtablevideos to view them.

This box appears on the lower left corner of recipes that have video links

Videos by Tara Sgroi

APPETIZERS

Mommy's Stuffed Cabbage, page 22: How to fill and roll stuffed cabbage so that it stays tightly rolled for serving

FISH & DAIRY

Gnocchi di Casa, page 90: How to shape, cut, and cook gnocchi

MEAT, CHICKEN & MORE

Brined Turkey, page 128: How to brine and roast a turkey breast

SNACKS & SIDES

Pretzel Sausages, page 142: How to roll sausages in dough and parboil them before baking

Sea Salt Caramels, page 154: How to cook caramels; how to cut and wrap the candy

Granny Sweets, page 158: How to dip apples in prepared caramel (see above); how to top caramel apples with nuts

BREADS, CAKES & COOKIES

My Most Favorite White Flour Challah, page 182: How to braid 4-stranded challah and form round challos for Rosh Hashanah

Cannoncini, page 206: How to wrap dough around molds and fill baked horns with cream

Kaas Potjes, page 208: How to assemble cheese pockets, add filling, and grate dough for the topping

DESSERTS

Deconstructed Lemon Meringue Pie, page 246: How to make lemon curd and meringues, seed pomegranates and assemble dessert

Wähe — Swiss Fruit Tart, page 256: How to roll dough, lay out fruit, and complete tart

PESACH GUIDE

Adjust recipes as indicated in parentheses for use on Pesach.

APPETIZERS

SERVED
WITH STYLE

Ask my mom and she will eagerly tell you all about my early experiences as a "food stylist."

I was no more than nine years old when "bringing the tea" at the end of the meal officially became my job. A job well earned because of the many hours spent plating and decorating, whether with chocolates, dried fruit, or sugar cubes. Everyone always "ooohed" and "aaaahed" as each new creation appeared. No one, not once, mentioned the cold tea.

Food styling is what I do today, professionally. I really try to avoid the "what do you do" question at all costs. Describing my line of work usually requires a long and tedious explanation. I can't blame anyone; just a few years ago, I myself didn't know food styling was even "a thing." And if anyone would have told me that I'd be scouring antique stores looking (and even paying) for old, rusty, mismatched forks and knives, I would have laughed. But that's exactly what I do today, and I love every second of it.

We all become a bit like food stylists when plating, appetizers and desserts especially. The start and the end of a meal are impo   't of color, planning, and creativity will go a long way.

Try to visualize your dish and picture the p   u will use for serving. Once you know that, see if there's something to add interest (e, a dressing) and play around with it. Dishes don't need to match; use whatever you have, it all adds character. You can always add something to a dish that is boring: think colorful olives, store-bought sauce, whole grain mustard. All of these will add visual appeal.

Also, rely on greens, like Verdini Petit Greens (pictured above), as well as any other fresh produce, to elevate foods that are otherwise a bit blah. Just a handful is all you need. Look through the book and you will see all these ideas, implemented in a subtle way. You can do the same, in your own home, on your own dishes.

You can skip the rusty fork.

SWEET CHILI SALMON CUBES

I've been on the lookout for a fantastic appetizer for a while. It needed to be the type that could be prepared in advance, taste amazing at room temperature, and still look gorgeously elegant once plated. I thought I was asking for too much and kinda gave up. It seemed like it was going to be grilled chicken salad. Again. Then I met my new, friendly, and super talented neighbor, Yocheved. She introduced me to this amazing salmon and it's been love at first bite ever since. See? It always pays to be neighborly.

NOTES

This is a great Shabbos-day appetizer, as the fish will be flavorful and still moist. Bring the fish to room temperature before serving.

1½ pounds salmon, *cut into 1-inch cubes*

½ cup sweet chili sauce

¼ teaspoon cumin, *optional*

¼ teaspoon za'atar, *optional*

½ cup panko breadcrumbs

¼ cup everything spice

¼ cup breadcrumbs

3 Tablespoons black sesame seeds

1 teaspoon Montreal steak seasoning

2 medium zucchini

2 medium yellow squash

1. Place salmon cubes, sweet chili sauce, cumin, and za'atar into a resealable bag. Marinate in the refrigerator for up to 2 hours.

2. Preheat oven to 400°F. Line a baking sheet with parchment paper.

3. In a shallow dish, combine panko breadcrumbs, everything spice, breadcrumbs, black sesame seeds, and Montreal seasoning. Mix to combine. One by one, coat each salmon cube in the panko mixture. Place on prepared baking sheet. Bake for 6 minutes. Refrigerate until ready to use.

4. Using a vegetable peeler, carefully peel the zucchini lengthwise into long strips, making sure to leave some peel at the edges. You will get 4 to 5 nice strips on each side. Repeat with yellow squash. (Save remaining zucchini/squash for another use.)

5. Place squash strips into a microwave-safe bowl; microwave for 30-60 seconds. This will ensure that the strips are soft enough to fold without cracking, yet not entirely cooked. Refrigerate until ready to use.

6. **To assemble:** Fold one zucchini strip like an accordion, then thread onto a skewer. Next, thread on a salmon cube and a yellow squash accordion. Keep alternating between the yellow squash and zucchini between each salmon cube.

SEARED TUNA CUBES OVER KANI SALAD

I owe this recipe to Victoria Dwek, who first introduced me to seared tuna, done right. Until then I had never liked fresh tuna. Victoria taught me that I'd been killing my tuna by overcooking it. Tuna needs to be pink on the inside, and a quick sear is all it takes, but feel free to cook it to your liking.

HOW TO PREP THIS DISH TO SERVE ON YOM TOV

For the salad: Prepare the dressing. Refrigerate in a jar or cruet. Julienne the mango, the vegetables, and the kani. Place mango, veggies, and kani in separate containers lined with several sheets of paper towel. This will ensure that the vegetables won't get soggy. When ready to serve, assemble all the components.

For the tuna: On Yom Tov, I like to prepare the tuna earlier but sear it fresh, pretty much as soon as *Kiddush* is done. But, for Shabbos, or if you don't like to be busy till the last minute, you can definitely prepare it on Friday afternoon and leave at room temperature to serve at the evening *seudah*. Freshly seared tuna is always better, but it will be delicious this way, too. Just don't keep warm on a hot plate; that will ruin the fish.

NOTE

This appetizer works very well with the dressing for Sherry's Salad (page 46) used as a dipping sauce.

5 kani sticks
1 firm mango
1 carrot

FOR THE DRESSING
¼ cup mayonnaise
2 Tablespoons rice vinegar
1 teaspoon sugar
1 teaspoon chili powder
½ teaspoon paprika

FOR THE SEARED TUNA
2 tuna steaks, *1 inch thick, cut into cubes*
Montreal steak seasoning
2 Tablespoons spicy brown mustard

1 English cucumber
1 cup panko breadcrumbs

½ teaspoon grated fresh ginger
½ teaspoon salt
½ teaspoon crushed red pepper flakes
1 teaspoon soy sauce

about ¼ cup everything spice
about ¼ cup black and white sesame seeds
1 Tablespoon oil

1. **Prepare the salad:** Using a julienne peeler or by hand, shred the kani; julienne the mango, carrot, and cucumber.

2. Whisk together all the dressing ingredients. Toss with julienned ingredients. Place into individual bowls; top with panko breadcrumbs just before serving.

3. Sprinkle tuna with the Montreal steak seasoning. Smear with mustard. In a small bowl, combine everything spice and sesame seeds. Press all sides of the tuna into the mixture.

4. Preheat a griddle pan until nice and hot. Add a tablespoon of oil; sear tuna for about 1 minute per side, not more. Tuna should still be pink inside.

5. Serve salad with 3 cubes of seared tuna per serving; serve with dipping sauce (see Note), if desired.

SPICED MEAT ENVELOPES WITH VELVETY MUSHROOM SAUCE

This has become one of Casa Muller's go-to Yom Tov appetizers. It's the dish you have in the freezer that saves you from the oh-man-guests-showed-up-and-there's-nothing-to-serve. It's delicious. It freezes well. Kids love it (spicy! duh...). It bakes in about half an hour. It's not another potato knish.

Don't say I don't take care of you.

FOR THE MEAT FILLING

2 pounds extra lean ground beef

4 garlic cloves, *minced*

2 Tablespoons tomato paste

1 teaspoon salt

¼ teaspoon black pepper

½ teaspoon cumin

½ teaspoon paprika

½ teaspoon red pepper flakes

2-3 dashes cayenne pepper sauce (depending on how spicy you want it), *such as Red Hot*

30 (5 x 5-inch) puff pastry squares (3 packages)

1 egg, *lightly beaten, for egg wash*

FOR THE MUSHROOM DIPPING SAUCE

2 Tablespoons oil

3 onions, *thinly sliced*

20 ounces fresh mushrooms, *washed and sliced*

½ teaspoon salt

¼ teaspoon pepper

2 garlic cloves, *minced*

1 (8-ounce) cup nondairy creamer OR soy milk, *divided*

1. **Prepare the meat filling:** In a nonstick saucepan, brown meat over medium heat. Using a wooden spoon, stir and separate until meat crumbles and breaks apart. Add garlic, tomato paste, seasoning, and cayenne pepper sauce. Once combined, cover the pot; reduce heat to low. Simmer for 20 minutes, stirring from time to time. Taste and adjust seasoning/heat level to taste. Let cool.

2. **Meanwhile, prepare the mushroom dipping sauce:** Heat oil in a medium saucepan over medium heat. Add onions; sauté until translucent, stirring from time to time. Add mushrooms. Season with salt and pepper. Cover; reduce heat. Cook for about 30 minutes, until mushrooms are softened, stirring occasionally.

3. Remove from heat. Add garlic and half the nondairy creamer. Using an immersion blender, blend until desired consistency is reached (some like it smoother, some chunkier); add more nondairy creamer if you prefer it thinner. Taste; adjust seasoning. Refrigerate or freeze until ready to serve; rewarm over low heat.

4. **Prepare the meat envelopes:** Top each pastry square with one heaping tablespoon of filling. Bring together two opposite corners, then the other two corners, to form an envelope. "Glue" the edges together with egg wash so they don't open while baking.

5. Brush tops with remaining egg wash. Arrange on a parchment paper-lined baking sheet. (They may be frozen at this point..)

6. Preheat oven to 375 °F. Bake for 25–30 minutes, until golden. (If frozen, bake directly from the freezer after preheating the oven; increase baking time by about 10 minutes.) Serve immediately with the velvety mushroom sauce.

LIGHTLY BREADED SWEETBREADS

There are a few words that come to mind when just looking at these beauties. Elegant. New. Exquisite. The list goes on .... There's this misconception that sweetbreads are scary and difficult to cook. Nothing can be further from the truth. Sweetbreads are delicate, yes, but very manageable. This appetizer is a restaurant-grade delicacy that will wow your guests.

NOTE

These sweetbreads go really well together with this Horseradish Dipping Sauce: In a jar or cruet, combine ½ cup mayonnaise, 2 Tablespoons prepared white horseradish, juice of 1 lemon, 1 small garlic clove, minced, and 1 Tablespoon chopped fresh chives OR 1 teaspoon dried chives. Refrigerate until ready to plate. Serve a small amount of dipping sauce on each plate.

FOR THE SWEETBREADS

1 pound sweetbreads	dash pepper
2 eggs	1 cup fresh breadcrumbs
¼ teaspoon salt	oil, *for frying*
¼ teaspoon paprika	

1. Place sweetbreads into a 3-quart pot; cover with water. Bring to a boil. Reduce heat; simmer for 5 minutes. Drain off the water, add fresh cold water, and repeat. After the second simmering, drain sweetbreads and place under cold running water. Cut away any unsightly membranes or connecting tissue.

2. Place the sweetbreads into a pan that has been lined with several paper towels. Cover with a towel; refrigerate. At this point, sweetbreads can be refrigerated up to 24 hours.

3. In a small bowl, beat eggs with salt, paprika, and pepper (seasoning is kept to a minimum since sweetbreads are salty as it is). Dredge the sweetbreads in the egg mixture and quickly, very lightly toss in the breadcrumbs. The secret is to keep the coating as light as possible. In a large skillet, gently fry the breaded sweetbreads over low heat, until golden, about 4 minutes. Turn and fry the other side for an additional 4 minutes. Take care not to over-crisp.

4. Plate 3-4 sweetbreads over salad greens of your choice per serving, or serve over colorful carrots sliced thinly on a mandolin, as pictured. Serve with Horseradish Dipping Sauce (see Note).

MOMMY'S STUFFED CABBAGE

Mommy is famous for her stuffed cabbage. But she doesn't have an exact recipe ... it's more like a little bit of this and a little bit of that. One blissful summer afternoon, Mommy showed up at my house with three frozen heads of cabbage and six pounds of chopped meat. "Do you have some onions?" she inquired. I was overjoyed! Not only was I finally going to learn the secret to these beauties, but there was promise of a succulent dinner on the horizon.

Word spread fast. Requests for leftovers by hungry siblings instantly poured in. Everyone wanted a piece of the loot. Mommy patiently separated, mixed, diced, and rolled, all the while sharing tips and techniques that told of time and experience. I, in turn, watched and took notes, measured to the best of my ability while Mommy sprinkled, seasoned, and adjusted. The results were, as usual,

delightful. Thank you, Mommy, for taking the time to come down to Lakewood and patiently show me how this traditional Yom Tov "must have" is done. And most of all, thank you for giving us all a recipe we can cherish and follow.

This, like all stuffed cabbage recipes, is the evolution of recipes passed down from mother to daughter. My own mother-in-law received it from her mother-in-law, Bobbi Leitchu. She recalls waking up at dawn to watch and learn the secrets behind mixing the filling and rolling the cabbage. You, my dear readers, won't need to do any of that. You will be able to watch the video tutorial in the comfort of your home, and gain knowledge that speaks of generations, in minutes.

And the tradition lives on.

---

3 small cabbages, *plus additional shredded cabbage, not frozen, optional*

FOR THE FILLING

½ cup oil, plus oil for frying

6 onions, *diced small, divided*

4 garlic cloves, *minced*

1½ cups uncooked rice

2 Tablespoons paprika

¾ cup sugar

3 teaspoons chicken soup mix

1 teaspoon black pepper

6 pounds chopped meat

3 eggs

VIDEO TECHNIQUES

HOW TO FILL AND ROLL STUFFED CABBAGE

WWW.ARTSCROLL.COM/OURTABLEVIDEOS

1. As soon as you decide you might want to cook some stuffed cabbage, stick those cabbages into the freezer. The longer they sit in there, the better. Ideally, they should freeze for at least a week. This is the preferred method for peeling those leaves without breaking them. The freezing process softens the leaves, almost like cooking them, without the mess of the hot water and pot.

2. Remove cabbages from freezer and let defrost in large bowls or in a colander in the sink, as they will·emit lots of liquid. This might take a good few hours. Be patient.

3. **Prepare the filling:** Heat oil in a large saucepan over low heat. Add 3 onions and garlic. Cook over low heat until soft and translucent, stirring from time to time. Add rice, ½ cup oil, paprika, sugar, chicken soup mix, and black pepper. Mix to combine. Remove from heat; let cool.

4. Add meat and eggs to cooled mixture. Mix well to combine. Your filling is now ready.

5. Set out 3 (9 x 13-inch) roasting pans. Carefully, so that the softened leaves don't rip, peel cabbage leaves from the heads,

FOR THE SAUCE

2 (15-ounce) cans tomato sauce

1 cup duck sauce

3 cups brown sugar

4 Tablespoons chicken soup mix

2-3 Tablespoons lemon juice

See full-size photo on following page.

one by one. The bigger ones will have thicker membranes, or ribs, down the middle. Shave them down with a knife to facilitate rolling. Add cabbage pieces and stems to pans. Add remaining 3 onions. You can also add additional not frozen shredded cabbage to the pans, if your family, like mine, likes the cabbage pieces.

6. Place one heaping tablespoon of filling onto the center of each cabbage leaf. Roll the leaf around filling, tucking in the sides to secure. Fit filled rolls snugly into roasting pan over diced onions and cabbage.

7. **Prepare the sauce:** Combine tomato sauce, duck sauce, brown sugar, and chicken soup mix. Spread over cabbage rolls in each pan. The sauce will be thick. While cooking, the cabbage will release more liquid and the sauce will become gravy.

8. Cover pans; bake for 2½ hours. Remove from oven; add lemon juice to the sauce (taste and add more lemon juice if you prefer it more tangy). Return to oven for additional 1½ hours. Stuffed cabbage freezes very well, raw, baked, or half-baked.

NOTE

The smaller leaves yield the prettiest cabbage rolls. What to do with the larger leaves? You can rip them apart at the center by the membrane and use them for two rolls. Use the membrane as one edge and roll into a mini triangle, tucking in one side only. Or shred and add to the pan.

TIP

Here's a trick I learned from our trusted housekeeper, Galina: instead of freezing, wilt the cabbage by microwaving the entire head, wrapped tightly in plastic wrap. Microwave in 7-8-minute increments, removing the softened outer leaves after each, until leaves are soft enough to use.

OUR FAVORITE BATTER-FRIED CHICKEN

We reluctantly bring you the most amazing fried chicken recipe EVER. My kids don't really forgive me for publishing this.

This recipe was given to me years ago and has never left our repertoire. It's the type of dish that kids and adults alike love and look forward to. I save it for special occasions like Yom Tov and especially Chanukah, when deep-fried foods are something we celebrate. Your kids and guests will thank you. And nobody will miss the doughnuts, believe me.

Thank you, Rivki S., for sharing this recipe with us.

FOR THE BATTER

2 cups flour

1 teaspoon baking powder

2 teaspoons salt

2 Tablespoons paprika

1 cup water

4 eggs

1 cup cornflake crumbs, *optional*

oil, *for deep frying*

3-4 pounds chicken cutlets, *cut into long "fingers"*

FOR THE DIPPING SAUCE

¼ cup vinegar

¼ cup ketchup

¼-½ cup cold water

1 Tablespoon lemon juice

½ cup sugar

¼ cup brown sugar

1½ Tablespoons cornstarch dissolved in 2 Tablespoons water

1. **Prepare the batter:** In a large bowl, whisk together flour, baking powder, salt, and paprika until combined. Add water and eggs. Mix well until a batter forms. Add the chicken to the batter; mix well to dredge. Refrigerate the chicken until you are ready to fry.

2. **Prepare the dipping sauce:** In a small saucepan, combine all the ingredients except the cornstarch mixture. Bring to a simmer, stirring constantly until smooth. Add cornstarch mixture. Stir to combine, making sure no lumps remain.

3. In a medium-large pot, heat about 2 inches of oil. If you prefer, coat the chicken in the cornflake crumbs before frying; otherwise, simply fry with the batter coating. In our house, preferences are highly debatable; some kids (and adults) strongly prefer the coated chicken over the uncoated ones. Therefore, I usually prepare some of each, to satisfy everyone. Fry chicken until golden on both sides, 4-5 minutes total. Drain on paper towels.

4. Serve immediately with dipping sauce on the side. Sauce can be prepared in advance and rewarmed before serving.

THE ONLY GRILLED CHICKEN SALAD YOU'LL EVER NEED

I have a friend who I've been inviting for dinner for a while now, but she never showed. There was always a different excuse...until one day, I added, "We are having the grilled chicken salad tonight."

"The one with the red dressing?" came the immediate text message. "I'll be there at eight."

I knew that would do it.

FOR THE GRILLED CHICKEN

2 pounds chicken cutlets (not thinly sliced)

½ cup ketchup

½ cup mayonnaise

1 teaspoon sugar

1 teaspoon paprika

1 teaspoon salt

1 teaspoon garlic powder

dash black pepper

FOR THE SALAD

1 (8-ounce) bag chopped lettuce of your choice

1 mango, *cubed*

2 Granny Smith apples, *thinly sliced*

2 nectarines OR peaches, *thinly sliced*

FOR THE DRESSING

½ cup oil

⅓ cup ketchup

¼ cup vinegar

½ cup sugar

1 Tablespoon spicy brown mustard

1 teaspoon salt

1 teaspoon paprika

4 garlic cloves, *crushed*

1. **Prepare the chicken cutlets:** Chicken cutlets should be evenly thick, about ½ inch. If too thin, they may dry out. In a small bowl, combine ketchup, mayonnaise, sugar, and spices, mixing until smooth. Place cutlets and marinade into a resealable bag; marinate for at least a half-hour at room temperature. (If marinating longer, place bag into the refrigerator, up to one day ahead.

2. Preheat your grill, turning to the highest setting. Dip a folded paper towel into cooking oil, holding it with tongs. Wipe cooking grate carefully. This is my preferred method to ensure that the chicken releases easily from the grate.

3. Remove chicken from marinade. Place cutlets on the grill; reduce heat to medium-high, with lid open. After 3-4 minutes, flip cutlets (you should have nice grill marks by now). Reduce heat to medium. Close lid; grill for 5 minutes. This can also be done in a stovetop grill pan or in the oven; broil for about 7 minutes per side.

4. Meanwhile, combine all dressing ingredients in a jar or cruet; shake well to combine. Divide the lettuce between 4 dinner (or 6 appetizer) plates. Top with fruit.

5. Remove chicken from the grill. Slice cutlets on an angle. Top salads with the grilled chicken strips. Drizzle with dressing.

NOTE

Serve this salad as an appetizer or as a main. It's our favorite summertime dinner, light yet delicious.

Make sure to use fruit that is at its prime. Brush apples with lemon juice to prevent browning. The dressing stays fresh in the refrigerator for one week. We use it as a dip for crudités or over any salad.

CREAMY MOZZARELLA BALLS WITH SUGO DELLA NONNA

There's something so terribly compelling about these mozzarella balls. I mean, can you resist gooey warm cheese, enveloped in a thin crispy coating of more cheese and herbs? I didn't think so. These look and taste so delicate, yet they are a snap to prepare.

This serves as a great dairy appetizer when you are looking for a fun way to start a meal yet don't want to overfill your guests quite yet.

½ cup flour

1 egg

½ cup milk

½ cup panko breadcrumbs

½ cup grated Parmesan cheese

2 Tablespoons finely chopped fresh rosemary

salt and pepper to taste

1 (12-ounce) container mozzarella balls (such as cigliegine, made by Natural & Kosher)

oil, *for frying*

1. Set out three bowls. In the first one, place the flour. In the second one, use a fork to mix egg and milk until combined. In the third bowl, combine the panko breadcrumbs, Parmesan cheese, rosemary, salt, and pepper.

2. Working in batches, dip each mozzarella ball first into the flour, then into the egg, and finally into the crumb/cheese mixture.

3. Heat about 1 inch of oil in a skillet. Fry the balls over medium-low heat, about 1 minute per side, until golden. Handle balls gently and don't overcook them, or the cheese will start oozing out.

4. Carefully remove from pan; drain on paper towels. Serve immediately alongside Sugo Della Nonna (see page 92).

SOUPS
& SALADS

INSAPORIRE

insaporire (italian): to season; to flavor

Insaporire is a fundamental part of Italian cuisine. It is not merely the spicing, it is knowing when to add what, and for how long. It is getting your dish from being simply good to really great. Letting onions sauté long enough so that their natural sugars seep out and caramelize. Picking the right produce for the right season, even when everything is available, all year, everywhere. These are the many tricks one learns along the way, usually from watching a grandma cook rather than from reading a cookbook. It's what happens between the lines that is crucial. I find this especially true when it comes to soups.

I used to be intimidated by soups. Somehow, mine never seemed as flavorful as my mom's. Over the years, I learned and accumulated ways to *insaporire*. You will see what I mean when you read the recipes. Adding tomato sauce? That's one way of *insaporire*.

Growing up in a country where you can only rely on fresh ingredients taught me so much. Consommé powder was unheard of, prepared kosher foods a scant resource. Even today, my mom's spice cabinet consists of staples like salt, pepper, and paprika. You might find an array of different olive oils, but spices are kept to a minimum. She relies on fresh herbs, garlic, and lemons for flavor.

I find that so inspiring. Stroll through one of our enormous, ever-developing kosher supermarkets. You will find aisles of ready-made sauces, condiments, and shortcuts, not to mention ready-made foods. The comforts and practical aspects of all this do not elude me; sometimes I even rely on them, as would any mom of five. But there's always that little voice, in the back of my head, pushing me to stay genuine, to use ingredients I can name and pronounce. I know that anything can be flavored the right way, just by knowing how to highlight and bring forth the natural goodness that Hashem has bestowed in each edible that He created. All it takes is some time in the kitchen, patience and a bit of prayer while cooking. And a grandma to show you the ropes, always helps, for the gift of experience that she has, is one we have yet to achieve.

MUSHROOM BARLEY SOUP DONE RIGHT

P || FF || 12 SERVINGS/6 QUARTS

I know what you are thinking. Really? Mushroom Barley?

Hold it, hold it.

This is no ordinary Mushroom Barley Soup. This is Mushroom Barley Soup, done right. This is the kind of soup that will sit in my freezer all winter long, divided into small portions, so that Child A will be able to have some any time she wants, without having to wait too long for it to defrost. It's the perfect Motza'ei Shabbos, Erev Shabbos, before supper is ready, once supper is done, after homework, before bedtime, Sunday lunch, anytime really kinda soul food.

Yes. Now you understand.

NOTE

Why the tomato sauce, you might ask?

In the Butternut Squash Soup as well as in the Mushroom Barley Soup, I end by adding a can of tomato sauce. It's a trick I learned from my mother-in-law (told you, grandmothers always know). Tomato sauce will add depth and acidity, taking the natural vegetable flavor to the max. This is a trick that will help you avoid using MSG-laden additives.

Besides, it's the Italian in me. We add tomato sauce to practically anything.

3 large carrots, *peeled, cut into large chunks*

2 parsnips, *peeled, cut into large chunks*

2 Tablespoons oil

2 onions, *diced small*

5 garlic cloves, *minced*

1 knob celery root, *finely diced*

2 small zucchini, *finely diced*

1 small yellow squash, *finely diced*

7 celery stalks, *sliced*

10 ounces white button mushrooms, *sliced*

10 ounces baby bella mushrooms, *sliced*

½ cup barley, *rinsed*

2 teaspoons salt

¼ teaspoon pepper

½ teaspoon paprika

½ teaspoon garlic powder

2 Tablespoons flour

1 (15-ounce) can tomato sauce *(see Note)*

1. Place carrots and parsnips into the bowl of a food processor fitted with the "S" blade. Pulse a few times until vegetables are coarsely chopped (but don't let it run too long; you want small pieces, not puréed vegetables).

2. Heat oil in a large pot. Add onion and garlic; sauté onions until translucent. Add chopped carrots and parsnips, knob celery, zucchini, squash, celery, and mushrooms; sauté a few minutes longer. Add barley and spices. Cover with water; bring to a simmer. Once simmering, add flour; stir. Cook soup for about 1½ hours, or until barley is tender.

3. Add tomato sauce; stir to combine. Taste; adjust seasoning. Serve hot.

36 · OUR TABLE

CLASSIC CHICKEN SOUP

Chicken soup. The most unassuming, taken for granted food of all time.

What would our Shabbos table be like without this staple?

Over the years, I have collected many tricks and methods to achieve the most delicious and flavorful soup yet. Mastering chicken soup is not something I learned overnight, and still, it surprises me every time: When hosting, I serve a choice of fish and a restaurant-grade main course .... yet the chicken soup – that's the one that always steals the show. Without fail. Every week.

To be quite honest, I had no intention of including this recipe in my cookbook. Do we really need a recipe for chicken soup? Isn't that something every self-respecting Jewish girl knows how to cook just from breathing its aroma week after week? Apparently not. Many friends, upon hearing that I was working on a cookbook, requested that I spill the secret to my chicken soup.

And here's the scoop: There was never a secret. It's just some insaporire that I have developed, taking tips from Mommy and Ima, a neighbor, a friend.

1 (1½-2 lb) package chicken bones

3 turkey necks

4 chicken bottoms

1½ lb. second cut brisket (I usually use the pieces I trimmed from a roast)

½ lb. chicken gizzards, *if available*

4 large carrots (the thicker the carrot, the sweeter) *peeled*

3 onions, *peeled*

1 zucchini, *not peeled, ends trimmed*

2 parsnips, *peeled*

1 leek

4-5 stalks celery

5-6 garlic cloves

1 knob celery root, *peeled, cut into large chunks*

1 red pepper, *halved, with stem and seeds*

handful fresh dill

handful fresh parsley

2 Tablespoons salt

1 Tablespoon garlic powder

1 teaspoon paprika

½ teaspoon ground black pepper

1. Place all ingredients into a large (16-quart) pot, starting with chicken and bones, then the meat, ending with the vegetables and spices. Add water just to cover; bring to a gentle simmer. Cook for 3-4 hours.

2. Let cool. Once soup has cooled enough to handle, transfer vegetables, chicken bottoms, and meat to a smaller pot or container. Discard bones, herbs, and any vegetables you won't be serving (the only one I discard is the parsnip). Strain broth through a sieve into the pot or container.

3. Refrigerate overnight. Once fat has congealed over the soup, remove by adhering a thin plastic bag over the surface, making sure it covers entire surface and then lifting it off. Works every time.

4. Bring soup to boil; serve hot alongside some shredded brisket and the optional but highly recommended matzah ball, from your favorite recipe (not included).

BUTTERNUT SQUASH CREAM SOUP

This soup is always in our rotation. We never tire of it. Thick and silky, it's forever a favorite.

NOTE _____

This soup freezes well. When defrosting, re-blend using the immersion blender to restore creaminess.

Ever heard of black garlic? It is the newest hip thing to use. Try it in this soup. I add 2-3 cloves to give the soup that umami depth. It makes you stop and think, *What is this deliciousness I just tasted?* This is totally an extra that is not needed in the recipe per se, but well worth a try. If using, add the cloves in the last 10 minutes of cooking, and then blend.

2 Tablespoons oil

4 onions, *diced*

3 garlic cloves, *minced*

2 large butternut squash, *peeled and diced*

1 large knob celery root, *peeled and diced*

3 carrots, *peeled and diced*

1 Tablespoon salt OR Lawry's seasoned salt

¼ teaspoon pepper

½ teaspoon garlic powder

½ teaspoon paprika

1 (15-ounce) can tomato sauce

1. In a large pot, heat the oil. Add onions and garlic; sauté until onions are softened. Add butternut squash, knob celery, and carrots. Add the spices. Add water just to cover. Bring soup to a simmer; cook until butternut squash is fork tender, about 1 hour.

2. Blend soup until smooth, using an immersion blender. Add tomato sauce; blend again. Taste; adjust seasoning to your liking.

3. Serve hot with Malawach Pinwheels (see below), if desired.

MALAWACH PINWHEELS

1 (9-inch) disc Malawach dough, *defrosted*

1 heaping Tablespoon duck sauce

1 Tablespoon everything spice

NOTE _____

Pinwheels can also be frozen before baking; simply thaw and bake as directed in a preheated oven.

1. Preheat oven to 350°F. Line a baking sheet with parchment paper.

2. Roll out dough on a Silpat, aiming to get it as thin as possible. Smear with duck sauce; sprinkle with everything spice. Roll up tightly, jelly roll style. With a sharp knife, slice into ¼-inch thick rounds.

3. Lay rounds flat on prepared baking sheet; bake for 30 minutes. Serve at room temperature; can be prepared in advance and frozen. Allow to thaw before serving.

THE GREEN SOUP

The soups in our house are color-coded. It keeps things simple and secrets concealed. The secret being the vegetables, of course.

My boys give me a hard time when it comes to eating their veggies. With soups, though, I find I can get away with more.

"Why is the soup green?"

"Because green is one of your favorite colors, am I right?"

It worked back then. By now, he knows why it's green. But it's too late. He already loves green soup too much to argue.

NOTE

After defrosting, re-blend soup with the immersion blender to restore creaminess.

To make this soup completely carb free while not affecting its taste and wonderful creamy consistency, substitute red potatoes with 2 cups frozen cauliflower. It's just as good; even my pickiest eater doesn't notice the difference.

2 ripe tomatoes
2 Tablespoons oil
3 onions, *diced*
3 garlic cloves, *minced*
6-7 small zucchini, *scrubbed and diced*
2 small knob celery roots, *peeled and diced*
2 small red potatoes, *peeled and diced*
1 Tablespoon salt
¼ teaspoon pepper
½ teaspoon garlic powder

1. Mark a small x at the top of each tomato and place them into a small bowl. Cover tomatoes with boiling water. Set aside.

2. Heat oil in a large pot. Add onions and garlic; sauté. Meanwhile, carefully remove tomatoes from boiling water. Peel tomatoes; skin should come off easily. Finely dice peeled tomatoes; add to the sautéing onions, constantly stirring. Once the onions are soft, add remaining vegetables and spices.

3. Add water just to cover. Bring soup to a simmer; cook additional 45 minutes.

4. Blend soup until smooth, using an immersion blender. Serve with Crunchy Tortilla Strips, if desired.

CRUNCHY TORTILLA STRIPS

1 package yellow flour tortillas
oil, *for frying*
salt

1. Cut tortillas into strips. This can be done easily by layering and cutting a few tortillas at the time.

2. In a frying pan, heat a generous layer of oil. Fry the tortilla strips, in batches, until golden. Using a slotted spoon, transfer to a plate lined with paper towels. Sprinkle with salt. Tortilla strips can be prepared in advance and stored in an airtight container.

MRS. BERNFELD'S SPLIT PEA SOUP WITH NOCKERLACH

Certain soups are better if cooked by Bubbies. And those Bubbies usually separate that massive pot of said steaming fresh soup into the many containers, for the many waiting grandchildren. And the grandchildren show up to pick up said soup with eager, happy faces, and sometimes even have a large bowl, right there and then, sitting on the stool at the counter.

Now, this is all well and good if you are one of the lucky aforementioned grandchildren. But, if you are not, here is what you do. You rely on recipes like these, that come directly from the Bubbie source and taste like Bubbie made them.

So thank you, Mrs. Bernfeld (or, dare I say, Bubbie Bernfeld?), for sharing secrets that only cooking many pots of soup can tell.

---

1 (1-pound) bag yellow split peas

2 Tablespoons oil

2 leeks, *thinly sliced*

3 onions, *diced*

5 cloves garlic, *minced*

3 carrots, *peeled, cut into large chunks*

2 parsnips, *peeled, cut into large chunks*

4 stalks celery, *cut into chunks*

½ cup barley

3 cubes frozen dill

3 cubes frozen parsley

1½ Tablespoons Lawry's seasoned salt OR kosher salt

1 Tablespoon garlic powder

1 teaspoon paprika

¼ teaspoon black pepper

FOR THE NOCKERLACH

3 eggs

1 cup flour

slightly less than ⅔ cup water

½ teaspoon salt

½ teaspoon baking powder

a bit more than 3 Tablespoons oil

1. Place split peas into a small pot; cover with water. Simmer until peas are mushy, almost a purée, about 45 minutes, adding water as needed and stirring occasionally so that peas don't burn.

2. Meanwhile, heat oil in a large (8-quart) pot; sauté leeks, onions, and garlic. Place carrots, parsnips, and celery into the bowl of a food processor fitted with the "S" blade. Pulse a few times until vegetables are coarsely chopped (don't run it too long; you want small pieces). Add to sautéed onions; stir. Sweat veggies for 20–30 minutes over low heat, stirring frequently to prevent burning.

3. Add about 8 cups of water to the pot; add barley, herbs, and spices. Cook on a low simmer for about 20 minutes.

4. Using an immersion blender, blend cooked split peas until smooth and silky. Add purée to the soup pot. Add water to cover; stir. Bring to a boil; cook for 1½–2 hours, stirring from time to time.

5. **Prepare the nockerlach (egg drops):** Combine ingredients until smooth. Refrigerate mixture for at least half an hour.

6. Dip a slotted spoon into boiling soup; use the hot spoon to scoop up about one tablespoon of batter; drop it into soup; repeat with remaining batter. Cook for ten minutes. Batter will be runny; it will separate into egg drops in the soup. You might not need all the batter; stop when you have enough nockerlach to your taste.

7. Adjust seasoning; add water if necessary. Serve hot.

SHERRY'S SALAD

D || 4 APPETIZERS OR 8 SIDE DISHES SERVINGS

Sherry is one of those friends who always pops up at your door with just the right thing at the right moment. Well, this salad is always just the right thing. And I'll take it at any given moment. The combination of flavors is so unique and refreshingly different, it feels like a little party going on in your mouth. We once prepared it for a school function and the next morning Sherry had 12 messages on her voicemail asking for the recipe.

YOM TOV PREP

Before Yom Tov, defrost and drain frozen spinach as directed. On Yom Tov, close to serving time, heat spinach in a saucepan until warm, making sure not to dry it out. Continue with recipe. Serve warm.

TIP

Use this great dressing as a dipping sauce for the Seared Tuna Cubes Over Kani Salad (page 16).

FOR THE DRESSING

½ cup mayonnaise

⅓ cup apricot jam

2 fresh garlic cloves, *minced*

2 Tablespoons teriyaki sauce

2 Tablespoons soy sauce

2-4 Tablespoons water

FOR THE SALAD

1 (16-ounce) bag frozen chopped spinach, *defrosted*

1 (8-ounce) bag assorted greens

handful fresh baby spinach

1 ripe mango, *cubed*

1 (8.8 ounce) package feta cheese

¼ cup shelled pistachio nuts

1. Prepare the dressing: Combine mayonnaise, apricot jam, garlic, teriyaki, and soy sauce in a blender or food processor. Pulse until creamy and smooth. Slowly add water, one tablespoon at a time, until you reach desired consistency. Dressing stays fresh in a tightly closed container for a week, refrigerated.

2. Heat spinach in a bowl in the microwave, until nice and warm, about 5 minutes. Squeeze out excess water. Set aside.

3. On 4 appetizer plates, arrange salad greens and baby spinach. Top with warm spinach, then cubed mango. Crumble feta cheese over salad. Sprinkle with pistachios; top with dressing, about one tablespoon per serving. You will have some leftover dressing. Alternatively, assemble in a large salad bowl to serve.

GOAT CHEESE CROQUETTE SALAD

I like to serve this salad as an appetizer. It's pretty, it's light, and most of it can be prepared in advance. Plate each salad, dressed, and add the warm croquettes just before the guests arrive.

TIP

Worried that the plated apples will turn brown? Simply brushing them with a bit of freshly squeezed lemon juice will take care of that. And it'll add a welcome hint of flavor.

1 (7.05 ounce) goat cheese log

1 egg

1 egg yolk

½ cup panko breadcrumbs

½ cup chopped pistachio nuts

nonstick cooking spray

1 (8-ounce) bag mixed greens

1 Granny Smith apple, *cut into slivers*

1 cup red grapes, *sliced lengthwise*

¼ cup pecans

FOR THE DRESSING

2 Tablespoons honey

juice and zest of 1 lemon

4 Tablespoons balsamic vinegar

1. Cut goat cheese log into 8 rounds (each approximately ¼-inch thick). In a small bowl, whisk together egg and yolk. In another bowl, combine panko and pistachios. One by one, press goat cheese rounds into panko mixture, then dip into egg, then again in panko. Press in well. Cover and freeze for at least 30 minutes or more if preparing in advance.

2. **Prepare the dressing:** Combine honey, lemon juice, zest, and vinegar, in a jar or cruet. Shake to combine. Dressing can be prepared and refrigerated in a tightly closed container for up to 5 days.

3. Arrange greens on 4 appetizer plates. Top with apples (see Tip), grapes, and pecans. Drizzle lightly with dressing, about 1 tablespoon per serving.

4. About 30 minutes before guests arrive: Heat skillet over medium heat. Spray lightly with nonstick cooking spray. Fry croquettes over low heat, 6-10 minutes per side, or until you see cheese is melted inside when pricked with a fork. Be patient — the croquettes cook slowly! If you try to hurry it, the result will be burnt coating and cold cheese filling.

5. Lower heat to a minimum and keep croquettes warm until all guests are present and ready to eat. Top each salad with two croquettes.

BROWN BUTTERED PEAR SALAD

Who said winter salads ought to be boring? Nonsense. Show up at your next family Melave Malka with a big bowl of Brown Buttered Pear Salad and steal the show. The salty Parmesan combined with the sweetness of the warm, buttered pears will have your taste buds singing and everyone talking.

What is brown butter? Brown butter happens when you let butter melt and caramelize. Be patient and keep swirling that pan with the melting butter, and no, you are not ruining it. When it literally turns brown, you'll know that that's when the magic happens. The butter develops a nutty, deep flavor that enhances the sweetness of the fruit.

2 Tablespoons butter

dash salt

freshly ground black pepper

2 Tablespoons sugar

2 Bosc pears, *cored and sliced lengthwise*

8 cups mixed greens (some arugula works well here too)

½ cup walnuts, *chopped*

½ cup thinly shaved Parmesan cheese

FOR THE DRESSING

¼ cup white wine vinegar

2 Tablespoons honey

2 teaspoons mustard

juice of one lemon

½ teaspoon salt

½ teaspoon pepper

½ cup extra virgin olive oil

1 heaping Tablespoon mayonnaise

1. Heat a large frying pan over high heat. Once hot, drop in the butter; lower heat to medium. Butter will melt quickly and start browning. Swirl the pan round and round, ensuring even browning. Once butter is brown, add salt and pepper (about three grinds of black pepper). Sprinkle sugar over prepared pears; toss to distribute evenly. Add pears to the pan; gently toss to coat in butter. Sauté over low heat until pears are slightly caramelized and just starting to soften.

2. **Meanwhile, prepare the dressing:** In a blender, combine vinegar, honey, mustard, lemon juice, salt, and pepper. Pulse to combine. With the blender running, add olive oil in a slow stream. Lastly, add the mayonnaise and let the machine run until dressing is smooth.

3. Toss the greens with the walnuts. Top with the caramelized pears and shaved Parmesan cheese. Drizzle with dressing just before serving.

ROASTED BEET AND GOAT CHEESE SALAD

This salad is pretty, refreshing, and light. Perfect to serve alongside a dairy meal.

Don't omit that teaspoon of toasted sesame oil — it makes all the difference. The nutty flavor of the oil balances the goat cheese.

NOTE

Use red and golden beets, if available, for a striking presentation.

3-4 medium beets (see Note)
½ (7.05-ounce) goat cheese log, *crumbled*

4 cups assorted greens (I use a mix of radicchio, arugula, and baby spinach)
¼ cup shelled pistachio nuts

FOR THE DRESSING

¼ cup oil
¼ cup vinegar
1 Tablespoon honey

1 teaspoon Dijon mustard
1 teaspoon toasted sesame oil

1. Preheat oven to 375°F. Wrap each beet in heavy-duty aluminum foil. Place beets into a baking pan; roast for about 1 hour. Beets are ready when they can be pierced with a fork. Let cool. (You can do this step ahead of time. Roasted beets will stay fresh, refrigerated, for 3 to 4 days.)

2. Unwrap beets. Peel beets; slice into thin rounds.

3. In a large bowl or individual serving bowls, add lettuce. Top with sliced beets and pistachios. Add the crumbled goat cheese last to ensure the beet color doesn't bleed onto it.

4. **Prepare the dressing:** In a small bowl, combine oil, vinegar, honey, mustard, and toasted sesame oil. Drizzle over salad.

LUNCH IN A BOWL

A well-balanced lunch, I have discovered, consists of 1 carbohydrate, 1 protein, 1 fat, 1 fruit and lots of veggies. One day, headed to a full day on the road, I created this salad on a whim, hoping it would keep me full for those many hours away from home. The combination was such a hit, I started preparing it every time I was headed out, and slowly my friends started requesting it too. It is really filling and delicious at the same time. Because I don't include a dressing, I have the leniency to add the avocado (fat) and once mixed, the salad gets dressed as it is, with the creaminess of the avocado and the saltiness of the feta. I like layering it as shown in the photo; that way the lettuce does not get soggy.

It was a long summer, with lots of road trips, but I never tired of my healthy and filling "lunch in a bowl." It's a keeper.

⅓ cup crumbled light feta cheese OR cottage cheese, *drained*

2 Tablespoons diced red onion

juice of one lemon

⅓ cup cooked quinoa

3 cups assorted greens

⅓ avocado, *cubed*

½ cup sliced strawberries OR pears

1. Place the feta cheese into a container/bowl. Top with diced onion. Cover with lemon juice (the lemon juice prevents the onion from becoming bitter).

2. Add a layer of quinoa, followed by the greens, avocado, and strawberries. This method works well to keep everything crisp and fresh.

3. Toss well before digging in.

NOTE

You don't need to take out a pot each time you want some quinoa. Keep a container of plain cooked quinoa in your fridge for a quick, filling, and healthful addition to your salad each day. It'll stay fresh for about a week.

FRICO SALAD WITH CANDIED SWEET POTATOES

This salad is extremely risky. The risk consists of the fact that it is not certain it will get to the "finish line" at all. Whenever I prepare the different elements for this salad, I find bits and pieces just ... disappearing. The fricos are so tempting and crunchy. The candied sweet potatoes are just what their name claims them to be. So yes, consider yourself warned. You might want to prepare it while no one is around.

Frico is an Italian dish, known here as a cheese crisp. Basically, it's baked cheese that has become crispy. As a perfect addition to salads, it brings flavor and crunch ... and some novelty. It is easy to prepare, yet doesn't look it. Don't you love those?

NOTE

If your fricos break, don't worry. Just break them up further and scatter them over the salad. They are delicious either way.

PLATING TIP

If plating as an appetizer, divide salad among individual salad plates, drizzle with dressing, and top each with 2 fricos.

FOR THE FRICOS

1 (5-ounce) container shredded Parmesan cheese

FOR THE CANDIED SWEET POTATOES

2 cups finely diced sweet potato

2 Tablespoons olive oil

¼ cup silan (date honey)

¼ teaspoon paprika

salt

pepper

FOR THE SALAD

8 cups assorted greens

1 honeycrisp apple, *not peeled, sliced*

¼ cup chopped pecans

FOR THE DRESSING

¼ cup vinegar

¼ cup silan

2 Tablespoons mustard

2 Tablespoons mayonnaise

1. Preheat oven to 375°F. Line two baking sheets with parchment paper.

2. **Prepare the fricos:** Spray 8 small circles of nonstick cooking spray on one prepared baking sheet. On each circle, scatter some Parmesan cheese, making sure it is in one even layer. Bake 8 minutes, or until fricos are almost golden and crisp. Let cool. Transfer to a container; repeat with remaining Parmesan.

3. **Prepare the sweet potatoes:** Toss sweet potatoes with oil, silan, and spices. Roast on second prepared baking sheet, uncovered, for 1½ hours, stirring every 30 minutes, until softened and starting to char. (You can see a photo of the sweet potatoes on page 32.)

4. **Prepare the dressing:** Combine dressing ingredients in a jar or cruet; mix well.

5. In a large bowl, combine greens, apple, pecans, and candied sweet potatoes. Drizzle with dressing. Top with fricos.

ROASTED PEPPERS AND PORTABELLA MUSHROOM SALAD

There are certain homes where this salad is my "ticket in." Always a favorite, it is requested again and again.

I like to serve this salad warm alongside the fish course, sometimes even as a garnish over some lightly baked tilapia or salmon. It works well with meats, too, or over crunchy artisanal flatbreads, as pictured.

Any way you serve it, it will be the hit of your meal.

NOTE

This salad is incredibly flavorful. It will stay fresh in the fridge for a good week, which makes it great for Yom Tov. It's best served warm, but room temperature will do, too.

6 red bell peppers, *halved and cored*

6 portabella mushrooms, *cleaned and sliced*

olive oil

soy sauce

FOR THE DRESSING

7-8 scallions, *sliced*

½ cup sugar

⅓ cup vinegar

2 teaspoons olive oil

3 Tablespoons spicy brown mustard

10 cloves fresh garlic, *crushed (do not substitute with frozen cubes)*

reserved pan juice

1. Preheat oven to 350°F.

2. Arrange peppers in a roasting pan, skin-side up. Drizzle liberally with olive oil and soy sauce. Cover; bake for 45 minutes. Uncover; continue baking till slightly charred, about 20 minutes. Remove from oven, cover tightly, and let rest for 30 minutes. This will ensure that the peppers will be easy to peel.

3. Carefully remove pepper peel; discard peel. Slice peppers into long, even strips. Reserve ½ cup of pan juices. Set aside.

4. Place mushrooms into a roasting pan; drizzle liberally with olive oil and soy sauce. Cover; bake for 45 minutes, stirring occasionally. (You can bake mushrooms and peppers simultaneously.)

5. Combine dressing ingredients with peppers and mushrooms. Serve warm.

CRUNCHY ASIAN SALAD

The credit for this unique salad goes to my dear friend Debbie L. We've been friends since we were 15, and somehow, our best memories together always involve some form of great food. As you can see, nothing's changed.

This is the type of salad that will become a staple at your Shabbos table. Beware, once you try it, your kids, and especially your husband, will request it. Not quite sure what it is, but there's something men like about this particular salad.

I like to double the crunchy topping ingredients and store the topping in an airtight container for future use. Once that part is done, the salad is really a snap to prepare.

MAKE AHEAD

As I specified in the recipe, it's best if you add the crunchy topping right before serving, but I have tested this salad countless times and the leftovers are great too. Yes, the crunch will be gone, but the flavors are still there. Actually, my sister just mentioned to me that she prefers this salad "the next day."

1 (16-ounce) bag shredded green cabbage

1 scallion, *sliced*

1 leek, *cleaned and thinly sliced, light green parts only (discard white and dark green parts)*

FOR THE CRUNCHY TOPPING

1 cup sunflower seeds

1 cup sliced almonds (with the peel)

3 Tablespoons canola oil

1 (8.8-ounce) package Israeli couscous (I use Osem)

FOR THE DRESSING

¼ cup soy sauce

¼ cup rice vinegar

¼ cup oil

¼ cup sugar

1. **Prepare the crunchy topping:** Preheat oven to 350°F. On two separate cookie sheets, spread sunflower seeds and sliced almonds. Roast for 15 minutes, or until golden, stirring them once or twice. Watch seeds and almonds carefully, they go from golden to burnt rather fast. Remove from oven and let cool.

2. In a heavy-bottomed pot, heat oil; add couscous. Stirring constantly, cook over medium heat till couscous is light brown, 10-15 minutes. (The couscous are part of the crunchy element of this salad, so don't add water.) Transfer to a dish that has been lined with paper towels. Pat off as much oil as possible. Add seeds and almonds. Store in an airtight container until ready to serve.

3. **Prepare the dressing:** Combine dressing ingredients.

4. Pour over cabbage, scallions, and leek. Mix well.

5. Just before serving, add crunchy topping, to taste. (The toasted couscous will soften slightly in the dressing.) Toss together; serve.

BALSAMIC TOMATO MUSHROOM SALAD

There won't be a Friday-night seudah in Casa Muller without this salad.

Child D, my second to youngest, is convinced that Tomato Mushroom Salad is part of the traditional Shabbos menu, right after the gefilte fish and before the golden chicken soup. She's never seen a different menu.

I once shlepped a bottle of balsamic vinegar all the way from Lakewood, New Jersey to St. Moritz, Switzerland. Three Shabbosim without Mushroom Salad?!? Unheard of. Impossible.

Boy, did I wrap that bottle well. And while unpacking, I silently said a (not so) little prayer, asking for a whole bottle, intact and unscathed. The things we do for our children.....

Ironically, when it came time to actually write down the recipe, I was lost. It's one of those: a little bit of this and a little bit of that ... and as a result, one of the table topics is always, "How did the salad come out this week?" It's never exactly the same.

I literally had to watch my mother-in-law put it together (she's the source for this unique dish). And now we have an exact recipe. Although my kids still say that Bubby's is better.

Sigh.

I try.

8 ounces white button mushrooms, *peeled and sliced*

3 medium good-quality tomatoes, *sliced* OR about 2 cups cherry tomatoes, *quartered*

2 scallions, *chopped*

2 Tablespoons olive oil

3 Tablespoons balsamic vinegar (I prefer Bartenura brand)

¼ cup sugar (you can substitute with sweetener)

½ teaspoon salt

¼ teaspoon garlic pepper

1 teaspoon Italian seasoning

1. In a large bowl, combine mushrooms, tomatoes, and scallions. Add olive oil, balsamic vinegar, sugar, and all seasonings.

2. Marinate for about 30 minutes, stirring from time to time, so that the mushrooms can soak up the flavor. Refrigerate if not using immediately.

TIP

This salad is great next to fish. I recommend using fresh mushrooms but in a pinch you can substitute with canned.

PLATING NOTE

For a beautiful presentation try using different-colored tomatoes, such as yellow and orange varieties.

NOTE

Garlic pepper is pepper that has been seasoned with garlic. you can substitute with ¼ teaspoon garlic powder and 1/8 teaspoon black pepper.

Italian seasoning is a mixture of dried thyme, rosemary, oregano, basil, and more.

TOASTED QUINOA AND EDAMAME SALAD

Quinoa and edamame are both considered "super foods" for their high fiber, protein, and magnesium content. Furthermore, quinoa is wheat free and gluten free. What could be better?

I love how the colors in this salad will give a face lift to any main dish that's a bit blah. You know what they say. We eat with our eyes.

NOTE

This salad is fantastic served right away, warm. It holds up very well too, for up to three days in the fridge. I find that the quinoa soaks up the dressing, so hold on to that extra dressing and use it if you feel it needs more the next day.

PRE-WASHED?

Fact-check the label when buying your quinoa. Try to get the type that is pre-washed; otherwise you will need to rinse it multiple times in a colander, to remove the saponins. Always toast quinoa after it's been rinsed and drained.

TIP

Prepare this salad for a "lunch-on-the-go," when you need to grab something substantial but neat enough to take along. It's healthful and filling. A perfect desk lunch. Desk lunches don't need to be sad anymore.

½ cup quinoa, *raw*

dash salt

1½ cups shelled edamame soybeans, *frozen*

1 red pepper, *cut into small dice*

1 small leek, *cleaned and sliced into thin strips, light green part only (discard white and green parts)*

1 Tablespoon capers, *rinsed and finely chopped, optional, but I highly recommend them*

¼ cup roasted, *salted sunflower seeds*

FOR THE DRESSING

1 Tablespoon extra virgin olive oil

1 Tablespoon rice vinegar

1 Tablespoon white wine vinegar

1 Tablespoon lemon juice

1 teaspoon spicy brown mustard

¾ teaspoon kosher salt

1 teaspoon sugar

pepper, *to taste*

1. Preheat oven to 350°F. Spread quinoa on a cookie sheet; toast for 8-10 minutes, till golden. Transfer quinoa to a saucepan, then add 1 cup of water and a dash of salt; bring to a boil. Reduce heat; simmer until all liquid is absorbed, 15-20 minutes.

2. Place edamame soybeans on a plate, cover loosely, and microwave for 2 minutes. (If it's covered too tightly, edamame will start peeling and lose its beauty, but will still be edible.)

3. Combine cooked quinoa, edamame, red pepper, and leek in a bowl. Add capers, if desired.

4. Combine dressing ingredients in a bowl or jar. Pour half the dressing over salad; toss together and taste. Add more dressing to taste, one tablespoon at the time.

5. Sprinkle salad with sunflower seeds before serving.

SOUPS & SALADS · 65

BROCCOLI WINTER SALAD WITH CREAMY ONION DRESSING

I'm pretty sure I have had this dressing in my fridge ever since that first bag of fresh broccoli made it to my kitchen. It just happens to blend perfectly with the vegetable and, really, any other salad combination. This salad is seriously divine (and you know me, I don't say that often). I'll prepare a huge bowl for dinner and, most nights, it rarely makes it to the table.

I'll never forget how Child D, age 3 at the time, looked at me with huge, horrified eyes the first time she saw me eating fresh broccoli. It was such a novelty – checked broccoli! – that I ripped the bag open as soon as I got home and proceeded to eat it like a bag of potato chips. Broccoli! Fresh! Kosher! With a hechsher! I was in heaven.

"Mommy, trees are yummy?" I guess I was munching with real gusto.

I noticed her lower lip quivering, her eyes getting bigger and bigger. Mommy was eating trees. Maybe Mommy was losing her mind. Scary things can happen in the life of a toddler. Mommy snacking on trees is definitely one of them.

"Trees can be very yummy. Especially broccoli trees. Here, have one." And it was love at first sight. She's been munching, dipping, and nibbling ever since.

1 (14-ounce) bag fresh broccoli, *larger florets cut into bite-size pieces*

1 (4-ounce) bag baby spinach leaves OR any other lettuce

1 large grapefruit, *supremed (see Note)*

1 cup pomegranate seeds

1 avocado, *cubed*

¼ cup roasted, salted cashews

FOR THE DRESSING

½ cup oil

½ small onion, *chopped*

3 Tablespoons honey

¼ cup vinegar

1 teaspoon mustard

½ teaspoon salt

1. In a large bowl, combine broccoli, spinach, grapefruit, pomegranate seeds, avocado, and cashews.

2. **Prepare the dressing:** Place all dressing ingredients into a jar. Blend with an immersion blender until creamy. Drizzle over salad right before serving.

See full-size photo on following page.

WHAT IS A SUPREMED GRAPEFRUIT AND HOW DO I DO THAT?

A supremed citrus fruit is one that supplies the flesh of the fruit only, no membranes, no pith, only perfect segments that will add a touch of elegance to your salad. It requires a little practice, but once you get the hang of it you will find yourself doing it quite often. Start by trimming off the stem end of the fruit, including about 1/4-inch of flesh, using a small sharp knife. Repeat with other end. Arrange fruit to sit flat on a work surface. Following the contour of the fruit, slice away the peel and white pith from top to bottom. You want to make sure the flesh is visible and you are left with no white pith. Working over a bowl or sink, hold the fruit in one hand. With your other hand, cut alongside one membrane and then alongside the adjacent membrane, releasing the supreme. Carefully transfer segments to a bowl. Repeat until all supremes are removed. Now you will be able to taste the fruit only, with no bitterness whatsoever. I find that even my pickiest eater will enjoy an otherwise daunting grapefruit, if served this way. Try it.

SOUPS & SALADS • 67

MASCHA'S CABBAGE SALAD

I have a sister-in-law who somehow always manages to come up with a new salad. Whenever we plan who's bringing what to family gatherings and such, it is always understood that Mascha will take care of the salad. Or knowing her, the salads.

This is one of my favorites, particularly because of how well it works with the Shabbos menu. Crunchy, colorful, with a perfectly balanced dressing.

TIP _____

To render this salad more dietetic, try substituting water for half the oil. It works.

NOTE _____

While vacationing in Switzerland one summer I discovered something quite interesting. Missing the convenience of pre-shredded cabbage, I was forced to use the real thing. Well guess what, "the real thing" (aka the whole cabbage head, which had to be cleaned and chopped by hand) is sooooo much better! What a difference! Tastier, crunchier ... it goes without saying that this is how I prepare this salad, ever since.

FOR THE DRESSING

½ cup oil

¼ cup vinegar

2 teaspoons mustard

1 heaping Tablespoon honey

1 Tablespoon sugar

1 teaspoon salt

FOR THE SALAD

4 cups romaine lettuce, *chopped small*

2 cups purple cabbage, *shredded*

2 cups green cabbage, *shredded*

2 cups broccoli florets, *chopped into small pieces*

½ cup honey-glazed pecans, *coarsely chopped*

5 scallions, *thinly sliced*

1. **Prepare the dressing:** Combine all dressing ingredients in a jar or cruet. Shake well until combined.

2. **Prepare the salad:** In a large bowl, toss together the lettuce, cabbage, broccoli, pecans and scallions.

3. Pour on prepared dressing just before serving.

CELERY ROOT AND WALNUT SLAW

Root celery, or knob celery, is linked to my earliest memories of Pesach; my grandfather used it as karpas. That tiny piece of root, dipped into the salt water, tasted more delicious than anything in our little, excited mouths. Until this day, whenever I peel vegetables for a chicken soup, I'll smell the knob and my mind will go back to those days at Zeidy's royal Seder table.

This recipe is my mother's, and it's sheer genius. Leave it to her to come up with such a great salad made with basic, humble ingredients that most of us would overlook. Although it's her staple Pesach recipe, we make it year round. It is surprisingly different, yet loved by all, kids and adults alike. The slaw pairs well with meats or chicken.

2 knob celery roots
2 Granny Smith apples
2 Tablespoons mayonnaise
juice of 1 lemon

2 Tablespoons sugar
1 teaspoon salt
½ cup chopped walnuts

1. Using the shredding blade on the food processor, shred celery root and apples.

2. In a large bowl, combine mayonnaise, lemon juice, sugar, and salt. Add celery root and apples; toss to combine.

3. Transfer to an airtight container; refrigerate until serving time.

4. Add walnuts just before serving.

See full-size photo on following page.

IMA'S COLESLAW

One Friday, I whipped up a few versions of Ima's Coleslaw (she will admit she makes it a few different ways). Then, I divided them into small containers and delivered them all over town. This one, using kohlrabi, was the hands-down winner.

2 kohlrabis, *shredded*
2 carrots, *shredded*
2 Tablespoons mayonnaise
1 Tablespoon sugar

2 Tablespoons vinegar
1-1½ teaspoons salt
½ teaspoon garlic powder

1. Combine all ingredients.

2. Place into an airtight container; refrigerate until serving time.

See full-size photo on following page.

GREENS WITH CREAMY BALSAMIC DRESSING

This is the only Pesach dressing you will ever need. My mother-in-law serves it with salad at every meal and there's never a leaf left. I strongly recommend using the No-Fail Mayonnaise, as we have tried to make this dressing using store-bought mayo but the results didn't compare. Feel free to add any vegetables/toppings your family enjoys. This dressing works well with almost anything.

4 cups assorted greens

1 cucumber, *peeled and diced*

½ red onion, *cut into thin strips*

¼ cup slivered almonds

FOR THE DRESSING

⅓ cup No-Fail Mayonnaise (see below)

1 teaspoon sugar

1-2 Tablespoons balsamic vinegar, *to taste*

1 Tablespoon water, *optional*

1. **Prepare the dressing:** In a small bowl, combine mayonnaise, sugar, and balsamic vinegar. Add water, to thin if desired. Whisk together until well emulsified.

2. In a large bowl, combine greens, cucumber, red onion, and almonds. Pour dressing over salad; toss to dress salad.

See full-size photo on following page.

NO-FAIL MAYONNAISE

My friends, let me introduce No-Fail Mayonnaise.

This recipe earned the "no fail" title after my helpful sisters tried it in their kitchens. The consistency is thick, just like the jarred stuff. The onions add a distinct, irresistible flavor. On Pesach, we spread it on everything, it's that good. My mother-in-law taught me this recipe, and I've been whipping it up ever since. Whenever three lonely yolks are lying around, mayonnaise ... happens.

3 egg yolks

2 Tablespoons finely chopped fresh onion

1½ cups canola oil, *divided*

1 teaspoon salt

dash pepper

2 Tablespoons sugar

1 Tablespoon lemon juice

1 Tablespoon white wine vinegar

1. In the bowl of a food processor fitted with the "S" blade, blend egg yolks and onion for 2 minutes.

2. With the machine running, add 1 cup oil in a very slow stream. With the machine running, add salt, pepper, sugar, lemon juice, and vinegar. Add remaining ½ cup oil; run machine 20 seconds. Mayonnaise will be thick and creamy. (Do not over-blend.)

3. Transfer to an airtight container; refrigerate immediately.

See full-size photo on following page.

LO MEIN

Do you have a recipe that is so delicious, yet so embarrassingly easy? And by that, I mean, so easy that you kinda pray no one will ever, ever ask you for the recipe? Because it really isn't a recipe? So to speak? Well, for me, that's how I feel about this lo mein. I received this recipe years ago from my sister-in-law Zeldy. She brought it over for the upsherin of one of my sons and I remember standing in my kitchen, after all the guests had left, fishing for the last few leftover noodles, wishing there were more.

NOTE

The best part of this recipe is the fact that it yields 2 9 x 13-inch pans. One for now, one to freeze for a future occasion. Yes, you read me right. This recipe freezes well. Just warm it in the oven at 350°F and stir well before serving. Alternatively, heat on a sterno.

2 pounds (2 boxes) whole wheat spaghetti

3 Tablespoons oil (preferably toasted sesame oil)

2 red onions, *sliced*

2 red peppers, *sliced lengthwise*

2 yellow peppers, *sliced lengthwise*

2 green peppers, *sliced lengthwise*

1 (15-ounce) can sliced mushrooms

1 (15-ounce) can baby corn

1 (10-ounce) bottle low sodium soy sauce

1 (10-ounce) bottle teriyaki sauce

1 teaspoon freshly grated ginger, *optional*

black and white sesame seeds, *for sprinkling*

1. Prepare pasta according to package directions. Drain and place into a large mixing bowl.

2. Heat oil in a medium pot. Add onions; sauté for 5 minutes. Add peppers; sauté until slightly softened (you don't want the peppers to be too soft or they will be limp).

3. Add sautéed peppers, mushrooms, baby corn, sauces, and ginger, if using, to the mixing bowl. Stir well; divide between 2 (9 x 13-inch) pans. Sprinkle with sesame seeds.

FISH
& DAIRY

———

POCO MA BUONO

The door is oh-so-heavy and big, but I manage to open it myself. I use my shoulders and my briefcase to push it enough so I can just about slip in. That massive door is called a *portone* (Italian: big door). It screeches a bit, and I know my mother will hear that sound all the way up to the second floor, and she'll know it's time to *buttare la pasta*, which literally means "toss the pasta." In the pot of boiling, salted water, of course. Not that we eat pasta every day (mostly every other day). It's just a way of saying "five minutes to eating time" in Italian, whether pasta is served or not.

I start the long way up the stairs, two at a time. I'm starving. Once I pass the first landing, I smell it. "Peperonata?? Can it be?" A spark of hope rises in my heart. And then doubt: "Can it be coming from the neighbors?" I hope not. My pace quickens and I literally fly up the remaining stairs.

I am a child. And nothing right now is more important than what's for dinner.

They say certain smells can arouse long-forgotten memories. How true. Whenever I cook up a pot of peperonata, I get seriously homesick. The scent of peppers and garlic caramelizing over a low flame whisks me back to my mom's inviting yellow kitchen. Peperonata was a staple dinner at our house. Lunch was the main meal, and dinner was small but satisfying: *poco ma buono*, little but good. Lots of things in Lugano, or Europe in general, are *poco ma buono*. Life is smaller there, but high in quality. People appreciate the little things, with an attention to detail that somehow escapes me here. When I visit, I marvel at how no one is running or rushing. Ever. They just seem to enjoy life, every minute of it, whether taking a leisurely stroll along the Lago di Lugano or hand-picking vegetables while chatting with the proud farmer who grew them. They have that luxury called time.

Which leads me to another example for you: the daily lunch routine.

My mom spent every morning first shopping for the ingredients, and then lovingly cooking our lunch. Lunch was our primary meal, punctually served at 12:30. We had to be back in school by 1:30, so there was no time to waste. My father came home at that time, too. My grandmother closed her store over the midday hours and went home to serve lunch to her husband. Most stores took that midday siesta. Yes, the world comes to a full halt in Europe; lunchtime is taken quite seriously. Families gather around the table and enjoy each other's company, children get to discuss their school day, and parents get to take a break from the office. All around one table. Sounds like a different world, and in many ways, it is.

And some days I do feel like I could use a little bit of that slow-paced "lunchtime therapy." That's when I will cook up a nice pot of peperonata.

Buon appetito!

LEMONY DILL SALMON

Do you have a Shabbos mental check list? I'm sure you do. You know, the one that goes, "challah, fish, soup, chicken, kugel, dessert ...." The basics. Well, let me tell you. Until a few years ago, that list always included the salmon. You know, the one that needed a pot, lots of assorted ingredients requiring peeling, slicing and dicing, an hour or so on the stove, cooling time, sorting time (yikes, is that fish juice leaking?!) .... Thankfully, that list got so much easier, all thanks to my wonderful sister-in-law Mascha. She introduced me to this incredible recipe, the one we never tire of. I've been making it for a while now – it's a keeper. It's so easy that the word "fish" has disappeared from my mental Shabbos list. And it never ever bores us. Quite the contrary, I always make a few extra slices so that Sunday lunch is taken care of.

But not only that; it's flavorful, pretty, and practical. You can serve it warm or cold, which makes it perfect for seudah shlishit. Try it and you'll see. Your Shabbos list is about to become so much simpler – and sophisticated at the same time.

You're welcome.

NOTE

If you cannot find the fresh dill, you can substitute with a sprinkle of dried herbs, such as parsley, chives, or dill.

4 (1¼-inch wide) slices salmon
salt and pepper
juice of 1 lemon
2 Tablespoons mayonnaise
2 Tablespoons ketchup
fresh dill, *to taste*
lemon slices for garnish, *optional*

1. Place salmon into a pan or oven-to-table casserole. (I like to use the Pyrex that comes with the cover, as you see in the picture.) Sprinkle with salt and pepper. Drizzle with the fresh lemon juice. Marinate for 10-15 minutes, until the color of the fish becomes lighter.

2. Preheat oven to 400°F.

3. In a small bowl, combine mayonnaise and ketchup. Using a pastry brush, brush salmon with mixture, coating evenly. You might not need the entire mixture; just make sure salmon is covered evenly on all sides. Top with fresh dill.

4. Bake salmon until fish flakes easily, 17-20 minutes, depending on size of slices. Serve warm, cold, or at room temperature.

SILAN, LEMON, AND MUSTARD SALMON

This recipe dates back to the days when silan was something you schlepped back from Israel wrapped in two sweaters and one towel in an already overweight suitcase. What? You don't bring spices, cheeses, and amazing ingredients back from the Holy Land? For those who do, this is how silan graced our tables for many years. Thankfully, silan is now widely available here. I use it anywhere honey is used, as it adds depth and interest to so many dishes. Drizzle it on your next yogurt and granola midmorning Sunday snack and get back to me.

4 (1¼ inch wide) salmon fillets

juice of 1 lemon

¼ cup silan (can be substituted with honey)

4 Tablespoons mustard

5 garlic cloves, *crushed*

1 Tablespoon olive oil

2 Tablespoons soy sauce

dash salt

dash black pepper

1. Preheat oven to 400°F (or if your oven has a "roast" feature, now is the time to use it). Place salmon fillets into a baking dish.

2. Combine remaining ingredients in a small bowl, mixing until uniform. Pour over salmon; marinate for 20 minutes. Using a spoon, baste the salmon.

3. Bake, uncovered, for 17-20 minutes (if using the "roast" feature, you will need no more than 17 minutes). Serve hot or, if refrigerated after baking, bring to room temperature to serve.

CHABLIS-INFUSED SALMON

When my dad declared he liked this salmon, I knew it must be special. My Abba never eats salmon. Too fishy, he claims. But this particular one, which my sister prepared last Pesach, he ~~liked~~ loved.

I recently asked her to kindly go to her Pesach kitchen (I know it's hard to do that in February, with chametz all over the place) and dig out this particular recipe. There was silence at the other end of the line, and then, "Uhm, actually, I don't know how to break this to you, but, since last Pesach, I prepare this salmon every week. It's not my Pesach salmon anymore, per se. I know it by heart."

"Even better," I told her. And I'm sure you will agree. A recipe that is so enjoyed, year round, without anyone getting tired of it, is sure to be a winner.

2 onions, *sliced into rings*

2 cups sugar

1 (750 ml) bottle Chablis white wine

1 Tablespoon whole black peppercorns

6-7 bay leaves, *optional*

juice of 1 lemon

4-5 (1¼-inch wide) slices salmon, *skin on*

dash salt, *optional*

1. Place sliced onions and sugar into a large, heavy-bottomed pot, over low heat. Stir until sugar is melted, then add all the Chablis. Add peppercorns and bay leaves. Cover; bring to a boil. Add lemon juice. Gently place the fish into the pot, skin side up. Bring to a gentle simmer; cook for 30-35 minutes, covered. Allow to cool.

2. After fish has cooled, transfer to a Pyrex container, skin side up (to help the fish stay flavorful and moist). Strain the pan liquids through a sieve; pour the strained liquid over the fish. Reserve some bay leaves to garnish your plates. Cover; refrigerate until ready to serve.

NOTE

Chablis is an inexpensive wine that gives this fish a great, foolproof taste. Your fish will always come out consistently good. Because there is no water, the measurements are always the same, no matter the size of the pot. I now buy a case of that wine and store it in my garage, for "fish use" alone.

CARAMELIZED ONION AND GOAT CHEESE TART

D || FF || 1 TART; 8 SERVINGS

This is not your typical quiche. Oh, no. This tart is irresistible and so perfect. Not too heavy or cheesy, with just the right amount of onion. Make sure you have company when serving this, because I cannot guarantee that you will not polish off the entire thing yourself.

FOR THE DOUGH

1¾ cups flour

pinch salt

¾ cup (1½ sticks/6 ounces) butter, *diced, chilled*

1 egg yolk

ice water, *plus more as needed*

FOR THE ONIONS

6 Tablespoons (3 ounces) butter

2 Tablespoons olive oil

6 large onions, *thinly sliced*

3 garlic cloves, *minced*

1 teaspoon fresh thyme OR ¼ teaspoon dried

salt, *to taste*

pepper, *to taste*

1 Tablespoon mustard, plus additional for brushing

FOR THE GOAT CHEESE SPREAD

4 ounces goat cheese

¼ cup heavy cream

1 egg

salt, *to taste*

pepper, *to taste*

1. **Prepare the dough:** In a food processor fitted with the "S" blade, pulse flour and salt just to combine. Add butter; pulse until mixture resembles bread crumbs (the colder the butter, the better). Add egg yolk and 2 teaspoons ice water. Pulse until dough starts clumping together, adding more water only if necessary. After dough clumps, remove from food processor; form into a ball. Wrap in plastic wrap; refrigerate for at least 30 minutes or overnight. Let dough sit for a bit at room temperature. Roll out and press into a tart pan. Run rolling pin over the edges and push all sides against the bottom and sides of the pan to seal well. Refrigerate dough for 30 minutes.

2. **Meanwhile, prepare the onions:** Melt butter with oil in a large pot over medium heat. Add onions, garlic, thyme, salt, pepper, and mustard; sauté until onions are deeply browned. Keep a close eye on the pot and stir frequently, as onions can burn easily. (Yes, the whole pot of onions will be reduced to almost nothing, but that's normal.)

3. Preheat oven to 375°F.

4. Remove pan from the refrigerator. Prick bottom of dough with a fork, then brush with additional mustard. Bake for 20 minutes, until slightly browned. Remove from oven; let cool. Do not turn off oven.

5. **For the goat cheese spread:** Combine all spread ingredients in a blender; process until creamy and smooth. Taste and adjust seasoning to your liking.

6. **To assemble:** Pour goat cheese spread into the cooled tart. Evenly spread the onions over the cheese spread. Return tart to oven for 25 minutes.

7. Let cool for a few minutes before serving.

GNOCCHI DI CASA

Have you ever tried preparing gnocchi yourself? You'll be surprised how easy it is and how delicious the results are. Gnocchi are a huge part of my childhood; they're my ultimate comfort food. Rolling the dough on the long, endless fast of Tishah B'Av gave some kind of solace to my hungry teenage stomach; I knew a great meal was on its way. Year after year, at times with my Nonna in the kitchen as well, we rolled and we sliced, three generations at one counter, talking and passing time, creating the memories I so cherish today.

This recipe includes Parmesan cheese in the dough itself, which renders the gnocchi super soft and tender.

NOTE

Gnocchi are freezer friendly, which is why many Italian women devote a day to rolling and prepping a large batch for later use. The best way to store gnocchi is by spreading them in one layer on a baking sheet and then freezing. Once frozen, transfer desired number of gnocchi to resealable bags and return to freezer. Thaw before cooking.

VIDEO TECHNIQUES

HOW TO SHAPE, CUT, AND COOK GNOCCHI

WWW.ARTSCROLL.COM/OURTABLEVIDEOS

5 pounds (approx.) russet potatoes

2 cups flour

1 cup grated Parmesan cheese

dash nutmeg

dash salt, *to taste*

dash pepper, *to taste*

1. Preheat oven to 350°F.

2. Wash and dry the potatoes. With a fork, prick them in a few spots. Place into a baking pan. Cover; bake until fork tender, about 2 hours. Once cool enough to handle, peel and chop.

3. Push the potatoes through a ricer or just mash them well. Weigh the mashed potatoes on a kitchen scale. You will need exactly 3 pounds. Refrigerate mashed potatoes, preferably overnight. The trick to great gnocchi is starting with cold mashed potatoes.

4. In a stand mixer fitted with the paddle attachment, at medium-low speed, combine flour, cheese, nutmeg, salt, and pepper. This can also be done by hand.

5. Add cold potatoes; mix at medium for 5 full minutes. It might look crumbly and as if it's not coming together, but be patient (and don't add any water!), it will form into a dough soon enough.

6. Remove the dough; divide into thirds. Shape each third into a fist-sized ball. Press out any air bubbles. Working with one third at a time, form into long strands by rolling the dough under your hands against the work surface (a bit like rolling challah strands, but much thinner). Cut the strands into 1-inch gnocchi, using a sharp, non-serrated knife. Use flour for rolling, as needed.

7. Bring a large pot of water to a boil.

8. Working in batches, place the gnocchi into boiling water to cook. The gnocchi are ready when the first ones rise to the top of the boiling water. Remove them from the water.

9. Serve with hot Sugo Della Nonna (page 92) and a generous dose of freshly grated Parmesan. *Buon appetito!*

SUGO DELLA NONNA

What is comfort food?

No one can decide that for you. After all, what does the trick for you isn't necessarily going to comfort your next door neighbor, right?

Well, for me it definitely is a bowl of pasta with lots of fresh, homemade sugo, just like my Nonna used to make it. Most of us will agree that the foods of our childhood are the ones that give us that warm fuzzy feeling inside. I am glad to see that Nonna's sugo has become my children's favorite too. I can see it in their content faces as they sit at Ima's kitchen table, feet dangling from the too-tall chairs, wiping their faces clean on a napkin that is definitely too delicate for their messy faces. I see myself, sitting at Nonna's table, as a child, feeling nourished and happy, just like they are.

The recipe is the same. The scene is the same. The feeling is too.

Sugo is Italian for sauce, and Nonna ... she's my beloved grandmother.

2 medium tomatoes on the vine (preferably Roma)

3 Tablespoons extra virgin olive oil

1 onion, *finely minced*

15 ounces tomato sauce

6 ounces tomato paste

1 teaspoon salt

2 Tablespoons sugar

black pepper, *to taste*

2 cloves garlic, *minced*

1 Tablespoon fresh basil, *minced (can substitute with frozen cubes)*

1. With a sharp knife, mark a small x at the top of each tomato. Place into a bowl; cover with boiling water. Let sit for approximately 15 minutes. The skins will start to curl up. Carefully remove from water. Peel tomatoes, core, and chop into small, even pieces. Set aside.

2. Sauté onion in olive oil until translucent. Add chopped tomatoes; stir occasionally while sautéing for about 5 minutes. Add tomato sauce, tomato paste, salt, sugar, and black pepper. Bring to a gentle boil, then simmer on the lowest heat possible for 30 minutes, stirring occasionally with a wooden spoon.

3. Add garlic and basil. Simmer for 5 minutes. Adjust seasoning to your liking. Serve over warm pasta.

NOTE

In a pinch, you can substitute a can of diced tomatoes for the fresh ones.

DAIRY OPTION

A traditional way to eat pasta is sprinkled with a generous amount of grated Parmesan or mozzarella cheese.

CRUSTLESS SPINACH & BABY BELLA QUICHE

You know that feeling when you remember you have something tucked away, in the back of the freezer, and you kind of breathe a mental sigh of relief? Like, I can handle anything now, I'm OK, I have something delicious and gourmet that I can put on the table.

This is how I feel about this quiche. I will prepare a few at a time and store them for emergencies, such as my in-laws popping in to say hi, or an impromptu melava malkah gathering. It will look like you slaved all day to prepare this quiche.

2 Tablespoons oil

3 leeks, *white and light green parts only, sliced thinly*

3 garlic cloves, *minced*

8 ounces chopped frozen spinach, *partially thawed*

10 baby bella mushrooms, *sliced*

¼ teaspoon salt

⅛ teaspoon black pepper

1 container cottage cheese, *small curd*

5 Tablespoons flour

1½ cups shredded Muenster cheese

3 eggs

1 Roma tomato, *sliced thinly into rounds, optional*

1. Preheat oven to 350°F.

2. In a large pot, sauté leeks and garlic in oil until translucent, 5-10 minutes.

3. Add spinach and mushrooms. Stir; cook additional 5-10 minutes.

4. Remove from heat. Add salt, pepper, cottage cheese, flour, Muenster cheese, and eggs; stir to combine.

5. Divide mixture between two pie plates or 8-10 single-portion ramekins. Decorate surface with the sliced tomato, gently pressing in slices.

6. Bake, uncovered, for 1 hour 15 minutes-1 hour 30 minutes, depending on size of dish (ramekins will need less time), until lightly browned and set. This quiche freezes very well. If freezing, bake for only 1 hour, let cool, and then freeze. There is no need to defrost; simply bake for 30-45 minutes before serving.

GOOD FOR YOU
PANCAKES

For years I thought of pancakes as a bad breakfast choice: white flour, sugar (lots of it) …. And all of that, fried, no less. Not my idea of a healthy way to start the day. But the kids kept begging for a "pancake breakfast," and like every good Yiddishe mama, I often relented. Until one day it hit me. Really, with the right ingredients, pancakes could actually be the perfect breakfast! Think of it: milk, eggs, whole wheat, oatmeal …! Could I actually get my kids to eat all of the above, hidden inside a kid-friendly pancake? Sounds way better to me than a bowl of cornflakes. So that's when the experimenting began. We tested, tweaked, and perfected until we settled on this recipe, which is a win-win situation – kids love 'em, moms allow 'em. Without the guilt.

Now we even do "pancake dinner," on occasion. Just don't tell my mother.

1½ cups milk

2 Tablespoons fresh lemon juice

1 cup whole wheat flour OR whole spelt flour OR white whole wheat flour

1 cup quick-cooking oats

2 Tablespoons (organic) sugar

2 teaspoons baking powder

1 teaspoon baking soda

1 teaspoon salt

2 teaspoons pure vanilla extract

4 Tablespoons oil

2 eggs

1. Combine milk and lemon juice. Let stand for 10 to 15 minutes, allowing milk to become "buttermilk."

2. Place all ingredients into blender. Add "buttermilk." Purée until smooth, scraping down sides as necessary.

3. Lightly oil a frying pan, preferably with cooking spray. Heat pan over medium heat. When pan is hot, pour batter into pan, using approximately ¼ cup per pancake. Flip pancakes when bottom is golden and bubbles form on the surface, 2-3 minutes. Repeat with rest of batter. Grease pan again only if necessary, between batches.

4. Serve immediately. Maple syrup optional.

NOTE

Combining milk and lemon juice gives you a form of homemade buttermilk. I liked that method, since most of us don't usually have buttermilk handy on any given morning. But, if you happen to have the buttermilk, definitely use it. Just measure out 1½ cups and skip the lemon juice.

MAKE AHEAD

You can refrigerate any leftover batter for the next day. Or, prepare the batter the night before and refrigerate, for a deliciously easy breakfast. Simply stir the batter and prepare the pancakes as instructed above.

BELGIAN BIRTHDAY WAFFLES

*Or Rosh Chodesh Waffles.
Also known as We Have
Special Guests for Lunch
Waffles. Sometimes called
Siyum Waffles. Rarely (but it
has happened) called Dinner
Waffles. Mostly just referred to
as Birthday Waffles.*

*You find the occasion. I will plug
in the waffle maker.*

*Thank you M.M., for getting
us an authentic gaufre (waffle)
recipe, all the way from
Belgium.*

½ cup sugar
1¼ cups flour
1 Tablespoon vanilla sugar
1 teaspoon baking powder

¾ stick butter, *melted*
½ cup milk
3 eggs

1. In a large bowl, combine sugar, flour, vanilla sugar, and baking powder. Add melted butter, milk, and eggs. Use a whisk to combine, mixing well. I recommend refrigerating the batter overnight for maximum flavor and texture, but it's not a must; waffles can be made immediately after mixing the batter.

2. Heat a waffle maker. Drop about ½ cup batter (depending on the size of your waffle maker) onto the hot griddle. Close the waffle maker; bake until golden, 5-6 minutes. Serve with maple syrup, chocolate sauce, or anything you like.

NOTE

Traditional Belgian waffles have sugar "pieces" added to the batter to add crunch and texture. I didn't include that in the recipe because it is hard to find where I live. But, if your grocery does sell pearled sugar, by all means add in ½ cup for the full "gaufres" experience.

MEAT, CHICKEN & MORE

———

WHAT'S COOKING?

"Maaaaaaaaaaa!! What's for supper???"

I am trying my best to teach these children of mine some basic manners. You know, the "Hello" or the "How was your day" that is expected from any person entering any home. I am so eager to hear it, I will even settle for a subtle "hey." I detest the "what's for supper" form of hello. And if I don't want my (very) future daughters-in-law to gang up on me and criticize the way I brought up these little men, I must act now. I've decided that discussing the supper menu, in the morning, is the best way to go about it. That way, the above-mentioned child comes home knowing what dinner awaits him and will, I hope, express some sort of civil greeting while stepping over the threshold.

So, we Mullers sit at the bus stop, sipping hot coffee or hot cocoa, discussing dinner menus. And that's how I came to discover something else. My children are actually open to more options. They are willing to try new things, if discussed prior. They are pleasantly agreeable in the morning. Vegetables aren't as daunting. Side dishes can be colorful. Who knew?!

And there's something nice about preparing a meal that has been "agreed upon" and discussed in advance. The children look forward to it and, hopefully, I will get a proper "Hello." Maybe even a quick kiss.

I know; now I'm pushing it.

"*A tavola!*" Dinner is served.

TANGY AND SUCCULENT LONDON BROIL

I often prepare this London broil for dinner to go over a salad. I like how low fat it is, yet so very high in flavor. Serving a delicious meat over a fresh salad makes you forget about the AWOL mashed potatoes or rice. Have you noticed? This is a filling meal and a satisfying one as well, for dieters or non-dieters.

One evening, while preparing this for my family, I noticed the meat looking particularly juicy and appealing so I snapped a quick picture and posted it on Instagram. My friends went crazy. "What is that?" and "Recipe please!" soon followed. There is something about the sight of rare meat that makes your mouth water. I know that's true for me.

I prepare a London broil more often than not. It's my Shabbos day staple, served alongside a crisp salad. That is, if it has survived the usual Friday traffic of hungry little people wondering what that awesome smell is.

1 (approx. 2-pound) London broil

2 Tablespoons balsamic vinegar

4 Tablespoons soy sauce

2 Tablespoons fish-free Worcestershire sauce

¼ cup oil

6 garlic cloves, *crushed*

½ teaspoon black pepper

1 Tablespoon mustard

½ teaspoon hot pepper flakes

2 Tablespoons honey

1. Rinse meat under running water. Place into a large resealable bag. Combine remaining ingredients; pour into the bag. Seal; marinate overnight in the refrigerator, turning over once or twice.

2. Set oven to broil. Place meat and marinade into a baking pan. Broil 10-12 minutes per side (total of 20-24 minutes), depending on how rare you want it. Let stand for 10 minutes; then slice thin, the thinner the better. Serve straight up or over a salad.

NOTE

Sliced London broil can be served at room temperature too (for Shabbos). It is best to store the slices in a bit of the marinade/sauce and not rewarm. Rewarming might ruin the texture of the meat. Rather, let it reach room temperature before serving.

FRAGRANT STANDING RIB ROAST

I came up with this recipe one Erev Yom Tov when I was a newlywed and had splurged on a beautiful hunk of meat I saw at Epstein's butcher shop. I couldn't quite afford it, but I couldn't leave it there either; Yom Tov seemed like a good excuse to buy it. After much research and debate about how to cook this meat, we were not disappointed. The roast proved to be worth every penny, and many, many standing ribs later, I can attest that it's always a hit. Just the scent of the meat roasting in the oven will make your guests want to linger.

And so, every Erev Yom Tov without fail, I receive a few phone calls, emails, or text messages asking once again, "How exactly do you cook that unbelievable roast?" By now, it's a classic.

DON'T MAKE AHEAD

This roast should be served immediately, like a steak. Before Yom Tov, prepare and refrigerate the rub and then cook roast on Yom Tov. This is not a roast you can prepare in advance.

TIP

Tenting helps prevent the roast from drying out as it rests. Cut a piece of foil large enough to cover the roast in the pan. Fold foil in half; drape it over the meat. Don't press it onto the meat; let the foil rest lightly on top.

---

1 (4-6-pound) standing rib roast with bottom bones in

1 head fresh garlic (about 25 cloves), *crushed*

1 Tablespoon Pink Himalayan salt OR Lawry's seasoned salt (if not available, use kosher salt)

1 teaspoon paprika

1 teaspoon black pepper

1 Tablespoon dry rosemary, *optional but highly recommended*

3 Tablespoons oil

---

1. Before you unwrap the meat, make a note of the weight printed on the label. You'll need this to determine the cooking time.

2. In a small bowl, combine garlic, spices, rosemary, and oil to form a paste. Rub into the meat on all sides. Wrap the entire roast tightly with plastic wrap and then in foil. Refrigerate overnight, up to 24 hours. Before cooking, let roast come to room temperature for at least one hour — two hours for a larger roast (see Tip on page 111).

3. Preheat oven to 325°F. Unwrap the roast and place into a roasting pan, bones down (hence the term "standing rib roast"). Roast for 25-30 minutes per pound. (For example, a 4-pound roast will need 1 hour 40 minutes to 2 hours, depending on how rare you like it.)

4. Remove the roast from the oven; tent with foil (see Tip). Let stand for 10 to 15 minutes before carving.

See full-size photo on following page.

NOTE

Don't expect the bones on your roast to look like those in the photo; usually the bones are cut short, but Mr. Epstein left these long so the roast would look so dramatic in the picture. You will notice that some roasts come with the bones removed yet still attached to the meat with twine or a net. This is because the roast is best cooked with the bones, yet slices easily without bones. Once cooked, discard bones.

ONION CRISPS

You know those amazing deep fried, crunchy onions that restaurants serve next to a succulent steak? Tell me one person who does not love those onions. I once ordered a bowl of them at a Manhattan restaurant, as an appetizer (no, they were not listed on the menu) (yes, the waiter thought I was quite odd).

I've been trying to replicate these onions for years, with different batters and such, ranging from beer to eggs. This method proved to be the easiest. And the best. I just love when that happens. These onion crisps are highly addictive. And fattening. Don't say I didn't warn you. Last Sunday, as we were munching on them at our family BBQ, we tried to come up with an appropriate name for this crunchy and irresistible side.

"Funions?" said my cousin.

"Onion Fries?" said my son.

Then someone said "Heartburn," and we all had a good laugh.

2 cups soy milk

3 Tablespoons vinegar

2 large onions

about 4 cups of flour

1 teaspoon salt, *plus additional for sprinkling*

2 teaspoons garlic powder

1 teaspoon paprika

oil, *for frying*

1. In a bowl, combine soy milk and vinegar to create pareve "buttermilk." Let stand. Meanwhile, slice onions thinly, into half rings, the thinner the better. Place sliced onions into "buttermilk." Stir; refrigerate at least a half-hour or up to 4 hours. (Don't rush this step. It's important for the onions to sit in the liquid; that's what makes them soft.)

2. In a large bowl, combine flour and spices. In a large pot, heat oil. Meanwhile, working in batches, remove a handful of onions from the "buttermilk," and dredge them in the flour, coating evenly. Transfer each handful to a colander and toss to remove the extra flour.

3. In a deep pot or deep fryer, heat oil to 350°F. Drop coated onions into the hot oil; fry until golden, but not too dark, 4-5 minutes. Drain in paper towel-lined bowl; sprinkle with salt, to taste. Serve warm.

NOTES

Onion crisps can be rewarmed in the oven or re-fried briefly.

See additional photos on pages 109 and 112.

HERBED RACK OF VEAL

I will never forget the first time I brought this dish to the table. I walked in carrying the entire rack on a platter. Everyone froze. There was literally a moment of silence. Then everybody started speaking at once.

It all began when my husband decided to help me one Erev Succos about 10 years ago. He thought doing the meat shopping was a good place to start. He came home with literally half a cow. I kid you not. After I calmed down ("Where in the world are we going to store all this??? My freezer is full of challos and desserts!!!"), I noticed something. It was not a half a cow. It was a quarter cow and half a veal. And a duck. This was getting better and better. Now started the "I don't know how to

cook veal!" and "What am I doing with a duck?" serenade. At the moment, I couldn't see it, but really, my husband did me the biggest favor that day. He forced me to expand my horizons (no more roast roast roast) and learn how to cook different cuts of meat.

It was a learning experience. You will notice I didn't include a duck recipe in the book. Ahem. That one didn't fly, no pun intended. But, the rack of veal has become a favorite and there will not be a Yom Tov without it.

If you are looking to make a statement or to simply serve a delicious tender cut of meat that is so different yet so yomtovdig, this is it. You will not be disappointed. This dish never fails to amaze.

---

1 (2-4-pound) rack of veal, *frenched* (see Note)

approximately 2 Tablespoons oil

kosher salt

freshly ground black pepper

1 cup fresh breadcrumbs

3 Tablespoons spicy brown mustard, *divided*

1 Tablespoon chopped parsley

2 teaspoons dry rosemary

3 garlic cloves, *crushed*

1 egg yolk

1. Make sure your rack of veal is frenched (see Note). Weigh and mark weight if freezing.

2. Preheat oven to 400°F. Using a pastry brush, brush meat on both sides with the oil. Liberally sprinkle with salt and pepper. Place rack of veal on a baking sheet, bone-side down. Roast, uncovered, for 20 minutes. Remove from the oven; let cool a bit. Reduce oven temperature to 350°F.

3. In the meantime, combine breadcrumbs with 1 tablespoon mustard, herbs, garlic, and egg yolk, mixing well. Place crumb mixture into a large, shallow bowl.

4. Using a pastry brush, brush remaining mustard over the veal (like you did with the oil). Place the entire rack of veal into the bowl; press the crumb mixture onto the veal, leaving the bones exposed (see photos). Carefully return the veal to the pan, bone-side down; return to the oven. Calculate 13 minutes cooking time per pound (for medium-rare). For example, if your roast weighed 2.5 pounds, you will roast it now for about 33 minutes.

5. Remove veal from the oven; tent the entire pan with a large piece of heavy duty silver foil. Let the meat rest for 30 minutes,

tented (see Tip on page 106), before slicing. This is a very important step; do not skip it. Your meat is still cooking inside, and no, it will not get cold.

6. Bring to the table on a large platter, served with Onions Crisps (page 107), optional. Collect compliments and then slice into individual chops. The outer ones will be more well done, the ones closer to the center more rare, pleasing everyone at the table.

See full-size photo on following page.

NOTE _____

My trusted butcher, Epstein's in Lakewood, does a beautiful job frenching the rack of veal. But, if you are not lucky enough to have such a devoted butcher, you can really do it yourself. All you need to do is to clean between the protruding bones, with the help of a sharp knife, aiming to get off as much cartilage as possible.

TIP _____

Always make sure to let your meat come almost to room temperature prior to cooking. Calculate at least one hour — two hours for a larger cut. This step is imperative for precise cooking. Cooking a cold-from-the-fridge meat will yield inconsistent results.

FALL OFF THE BONE TENDER FLANKEN

The treadmill is a great place to pick up new recipes. Who knew?

This exquisite yet simple recipe was given to me by R.S. Rubin, a renowned cook in Lakewood. It was worth going to the gym that particular Sunday just to talk about cooking (what else?) and end up with a gem like this one.

This recipe is used year round, but is especially good for Pesach.

NOTE

This meat can be prepared in advance and rewarmed. This works for me. When the meat is cool, the fat congeals and can be removed easily.

3 onions, *peeled, sliced into rounds*

4 (¾-1 pound) bone-in flanken strips

1 cup orange juice

½ cup sugar

1 Tablespoon potato starch dissolved in ¼ cup cold water

1 teaspoon salt

¼ cup red wine

2 Tablespoons oil

1 teaspoon garlic powder, *optional*

1. Preheat oven to 300°F (no, this is not a typo; cooking at a low temperature is important). Arrange onions in one layer in a 9 x 13-inch pan. Top with flanken. Set aside.

2. In a saucepan, combine orange juice, sugar, dissolved potato starch, salt, wine, oil, and garlic powder. Bring to a simmer over medium heat, stirring constantly. Simmer until slightly thickened, 5-10 minutes.

3. Pour sauce over meat. Cover pan with two layers of heavy duty foil. Make sure it is sealed very well. Bake for 4½ hours.

SWEET AND TANGY SPARE RIBS

A friend once called me, asking for a meat recipe. "It has to be amazingly good and incredibly easy," she said. "I'm kidding," she then added, but I knew she really wasn't. And I had just the thing. Whenever I meet her husband, he makes sure to thank me, AGAIN, for "those awesome ribs." Where does it say that great dishes have to be long, hard, and complicated?

NOTE

I like to cool the ribs in the middle of the cooking process so I can remove the fat layer, but it's not a necessity. You can raise oven temperature, uncover meat, and proceed with the braising part immediately after the 3-hour slow roasting.

about 8 (1-inch-thick) spare ribs, *nicely marbled*

2½ cups duck sauce

1 cup water

2 Tablespoons teriyaki sauce

5 garlic cloves, *minced*

1 teaspoon paprika

2 Tablespoons dried onion flakes

1 Tablespoon salt

black pepper, *to taste*

1. Preheat oven to 350°F. In a baking pan, arrange ribs in one layer. In a medium bowl, combine duck sauce, water, teriyaki sauce, garlic, paprika, onion flakes, salt, and pepper. Pour over ribs. Cover tightly with foil; bake for 3 hours.

2. Let ribs cool; then refrigerate overnight.

3. Preheat oven to 375°F (use the "roast" setting, if available). Remove congealed fat layer from the ribs. Roast, uncovered, spooning sauce over the ribs once or twice, until ribs are braised and glistening, about 20 minutes.

LATTICE MINUTE ROAST

For as long as I can remember, my mother-in-law (and her sister-in-law, aka Tanta Esther) have been saving this very popular roast for Yom Tov. The roast itself is incredibly flavorful and the latticed dough gives it just the perfect amount of oomph that a festive dish requires, without rendering it overly heavy. I asked Esther how long she cooks her roast and she replied, "Oh, I'm not quite sure. I do the fork test after a couple of hours." So I did that too, and guess what, it worked. Further details below.

1 (approx. 4-pound) minute roast

FOR THE MARINADE

2½ Tablespoons vinegar

2 cups duck sauce

½ cup soy sauce

5 garlic cloves, *minced*

1 teaspoon ginger, *minced, OR ½ teaspoon dried*

½ teaspoon dry mustard

1 cup sweet red wine, *such as Malaga*

1 (17-ounce) package flaky dough

1 egg, *beaten, for egg wash*

NOTE

After cutting out the lattice, you can re-roll the scraps of dough and form them into a ball. Roll out the dough again and shape it into a decorative bow and place it on top of the roast, just like my mother-in-law does.

1. Using a fork, prick roast all over its surface.

2. Combine all marinade ingredients in a resealable plastic bag. Add the roast; marinate overnight, or up to 24 hours, refrigerated.

3. Remove roast from the refrigerator; let come to room temperature. Preheat oven to 350°F. Place roast with marinade into a baking dish. Cover; bake for at least 3 hours, turning the meat halfway through the cooking time. After 3 hours, check the meat by pricking it with a fork. Meat should have softened and gravy formed from the marinade. If it has not softened quite yet, return to the oven for an additional half-hour, or until soft.

4. Remove roast from the oven; let cool, then refrigerate with its gravy. After fat has congealed, you can remove and discard it.

5. About 1 hour before you would like to serve the meat: Preheat oven to 375°F. Remove meat from the gravy. Pat dry with paper towels. Roll out the flaky dough; use a lattice cutter to form the lattice. Wrap the lattice over the roast, then place the roast, seam side down, in a roasting pan. (Alternatively, you can simply wrap the roast in the dough, no lattice necessary; it will be just as delicious.)

6. Add about 1 inch of gravy to the pan. Brush the lattice with egg wash. Bake until pastry is golden, about 30 minutes, basting with the sauce every 10 minutes or so. Slice and serve immediately.

ZAHAVA'S RIBS

In my phone's photo album there is a section called "Favorites." Among those favorite photos of toothless grinning toddlers and pudgy babies, there's a screenshot of a recipe Zahava Krohn once texted me, ages ago. It's there because too many times have I scrambled on a hectic Friday to find that recipe, and scrolling back 2 years' worth of texting conversations isn't exactly my idea of fun.

This particular one became a Shabbos staple. Elegant and delicious, easy and totally last-minute-proof (no, it's not a word), I am sure this will become a staple in your home as well.

English Ribs (or short ribs) are a cut of meat that is increasingly more attainable. They used to be a specialty Yom Tov item, but now practically every grocery meat department carries them. The first time I cooked them, my friend Chana Suri warned me, "Make sure you have a great bottle of red wine to serve along with it. It needs it." I didn't serve any wine that time, and we had no leftovers. But I know now what she meant.

This recipe works well with either English Ribs or short ribs. Intrinsically, they are the same piece of meat, just cut differently. It all depends how much meat you want to serve to each person.

(You can see the uncooked ribs in the photo on page 100.)

FOR THE MEAT

4 short ribs (I ask my butcher to cut the ribs into neat small rectangles, about 2 x 4 inches, but any size works)

1 large onion, *sliced*

coarse sea salt OR Himalayan Pink salt

freshly ground black pepper

½ teaspoon garlic powder

½ teaspoon espresso OR coffee powder

1 Tablespoon olive oil

FOR THE SAUCE

½ cup chili sauce OR ketchup (depending if you like it spicy or sweet)

¼ cup brown sugar

¼ cup red wine

2 Tablespoons dark corn syrup

1 Tablespoon fish-free Worcestershire sauce

1 teaspoon soy sauce

½ cup reserved juices from the meat

1. Preheat oven to 400°F. Arrange sliced onion in one layer in a baking dish. Place the meat over it, bone-side down. Liberally sprinkle with salt and pepper. Add garlic powder and coffee. Add olive oil; rub the mixture evenly into the meat. Cover tightly; bake for 2 hours.

2. Remove from the oven; pour off the juices, reserving ½ cup for the sauce.

3. **Prepare the sauce:** Combine sauce ingredients, mixing well. Turn ribs bone-side up; pour sauce over them. Return to oven; roast, uncovered, for 25-30 minutes.

NOTE

If serving on Friday night, refrigerate meat and sauce separately after cooking. Right before Shabbos, pour sauce over meat and place into oven, uncovered, on low heat until ready to serve. This can also be done on the *blech*.

WEEKDAY POT ROAST

Every Shabbos or Yom Tov I have the same exact thought process. It goes something like this:

Hmm, look at that.

My kids actually like meat. Roast in particular.

Well, after the leftovers are gone, and the week rolls in, I say to myself again, Why not prepare a simple pot roast for dinner? Maybe to celebrate a birthday, Rosh Chodesh, or a nice mark on a test?

It is such a comforting meal, enjoyed by all, especially in the cold winter months.

I like to use a chuck eye roast; I find it fairly inexpensive and very soft. Pair it with couscous or rice to soak up the sauce, and you have yourself a memorable meal.

1 (approx. 3-pound) chuck eye roast

kosher salt

black pepper

2 Tablespoons oil

3 onions, *sliced*

6 garlic cloves, *sliced*

1 small celery root, *peeled and cubed*

2 zucchini, *cubed*

1 cup baby bella mushrooms

2 carrots, *cubed*

1 (15-ounce) can tomato sauce

12 ounces (1 bottle) beer, *any variety*

1 ½ teaspoons salt

1 teaspoon paprika

dash black pepper

1-2 bay leaves, *optional*

1. Preheat oven to 350°F.

2. Preheat a Dutch oven over medium high heat. While the pot is heating, rinse and dry the roast well. Sprinkle roast with salt and pepper on all sides. Add oil to the pot; sear the roast on all sides until browned. Do not rush this process. You will know it's time to turn the roast when it releases easily.

3. Once roast has browned on all sides, set it on a plate. In the same pot, sauté onions, garlic, celery root, zucchini, mushrooms, and carrots until slightly softened. Return roast to the pot; top with tomato sauce, beer, spices, and bay leaves, if using.

4. Place a large piece of heavy duty foil over the pot and then secure the lid over it (this will ensure no steam escapes). Place into oven; bake for 1½ hours. Remove pot from oven; carefully turn the meat to the other side. Return roast to oven for an additional 1½ hours.

5. Slice roast and serve immediately, or chill the meat first to ensure easier slicing. Reheat in the oven or on the stovetop. Serve alongside couscous or rice, with the sauce (discard bay leaves) and vegetables.

PULLED FRENCH ROAST SLIDERS

I'll let you in on a little secret. This is actually the recipe for one of my favorite roasts. It's the one I tend to rely on when the going gets tough and I want a quick and easy recipe that will make everyone happy, me especially. It tastes great either way, as a pulled meat or as a roast, traditionally sliced.

This method of serving was "born" one day when my boys couldn't wait for the roast to cool and we sliced it hot. Left with an unsightly mess, we decided to serve this delicious meat over some leftover buns. And, as they say, the rest is history. I find kids will eat anything in the form of a sandwich, a burger bun especially, and for moms it's a dream dinner: no side dish to fuss with.

1 (3-pound or larger) French roast

3 onions, *sliced*

6 garlic cloves, *thinly sliced*

1½ cups duck sauce

1 (15-ounce) can tomato sauce

1 Tablespoon salt

1 Tablespoon garlic powder

1 teaspoon paprika

black pepper, *to taste*

½ cup red wine

16 slider buns

1. Preheat oven to 300°F. Arrange half the onions in a roasting pan. Place roast over the onions; top with remaining onions. Add garlic cloves, duck sauce, tomato sauce, salt, garlic powder, paprika, black pepper, and wine. Cover tightly; bake for 4-5 hours, turning once halfway through. Roast is ready when it feels soft when pricked with a fork.

2. Unlike when preparing a traditional roast, where the meat is chilled before slicing, pulling meat is quite the opposite. The hotter the meat, the easier it is to "pull." (If preparing in advance, simply rewarm before pulling.) Place the hot roast on a cutting board; use two forks to shred.

3. Using an immersion blender, blend the gravy until smooth. (If you prefer a thinner sauce, skip the blending and simply strain the gravy, leaving the onions behind.)

4. Place small mounds of meat onto each slider round. Top with a spoonful of gravy; serve.

MEAT MANICOTTI

All kids love meatballs and spaghetti, can we agree on that? And when we take an old classic and make it chic, we score super points. All of a sudden, the familiar, comforting flavors are presentable, even elegant. Oh, and here's the kicker: freezer-friendly! And you don't have to cook the manicotti first!

This recipe is now a staple in my family. It's the kind of thing we will send when someone had a baby or moved to a new house. Quick, easy, delicious. Perfect.

I traced the recipe back to its roots, and I owe many thanks to Faigy O. Also, thank you, Faigy, for taking the time to share with us all the little tips that make it easier to assemble this recipe.

THE LOW-CARB VERSION

I was once left with some extra filling and, you know how it goes, necessity is the mother of invention. I had a few zucchini in my veggie drawer and I came up with a great dietetic alternative. Cut each zucchini in half vertically, remove the stem ends, and then use an apple corer or a spoon to remove the core of the zucchini. Stuff the zucchini with the meat filling, place them into the pan alongside the manicotti, cover with the same sauce ... and ... voila! An almost perfectly carb-free dinner! Try it.

1 (8-ounce) box manicotti, *not cooked*

FOR THE FILLING

1 pound ground meat	½ teaspoon salt
1 egg	½ teaspoon paprika
3 Tablespoons ketchup	½ teaspoon garlic powder
½ cup cornflake crumbs	dash black pepper
1 small onion, *grated*	½ (15-ounce) can tomato soup

FOR THE SAUCE

1 (15-ounce) can tomato sauce	1 teaspoon garlic powder
1½ cans tomato soup	dash of pepper
¼ cup sugar	½ cup water

1. Preheat oven to 350°F.

2. **Prepare the filling:** In a medium bowl, combine filling ingredients. Working with one at a time, stuff each manicotti; place filled manicotti into a baking dish in one layer. (If freezing, do so at this point, without the sauce.)

3. **Prepare the sauce:** Combine sauce ingredients in a bowl. Refrigerate, covered, if preparing in advance.

4. Pour sauce over filled manicotti. Using a spoon, make sure the sauce flows between all the manicotti. If sauce doesn't flow to the edges of the pan, add some water at the corners of the pan.

5. Cover with foil; bake for 1 hour and 20 minutes. (You can assemble the manicotti and refrigerate until ready to bake, up to 24 hours in advance. Add the sauce just before baking. If manicotti were frozen, partially defrost before baking; do not defrost fully.)

BRINED TURKEY

I was kinda disappointed when I found out that my husband's family does not celebrate Thanksgiving. I was looking forward to some good, tender turkey. What's the point of marrying an American if it won't get me some turkey?! Jokes aside, my quest for turkey is real. And I finally learned how to cook a juicy piece of tender white lean meat, with incredible flavor.

I reckoned that dealing with the whole bird wasn't realistic, a turkey breast would have to do. Trust me when I say that sometimes, in the Muller household, dinner flops. With the turkey, it did, more than once. Fire alarms and drama included. Lesson learned: Turkey meat isn't naturally juicy.

And then, I had a breakthrough: brining.

Brining means soaking the meat or the chicken overnight in a mixture of salt water and some other goodies. The flesh absorbs moisture and renders a juicy piece of meat. Try it. It is easy and oh-so-flavorful.

This turkey is a Shabbos-day staple at Casa Muller; served cold or at room temperature, it gives that finishing touch to the traditional cholent course.

VIDEO TECHNIQUES

HOW TO BRINE AND ROAST A TURKEY BREAST

WWW.ARTSCROLL.COM/OURTABLEVIDEOS

1 (3-5 pound) whole turkey breast, *with skin, bone in*

FOR THE BRINE

2 cloves garlic, *minced*

½ teaspoon black pepper

2 Tablespoons fish-free Worcestershire sauce

1 Tablespoon brown sugar

8 cups water, *divided*

⅓ cup table salt (it dissolves more completely than kosher salt)

FOR THE RUB

2 Tablespoons mustard

1 Tablespoon oil

1 teaspoon garlic powder

freshly ground black pepper

1. **Prepare the brine:** In a large resealable bag, place garlic, black pepper, Worcestershire sauce, and brown sugar.

2. Bring 2 cups water to a boil.

3. Combine the salt with the hot water, stirring until salt is completely dissolved and no granules remain. Add salt water to the resealable bag. Add remaining water.

4. Place turkey breast into the bag; place the bag into a large baking dish to catch any possible spills or leaks. Marinate in the refrigerator for at least 8 hours or overnight.

5. Preheat oven to 425°F. Place a mesh wire rack (such as a cookie cooling rack) onto a cookie sheet. Remove turkey from the brine and pat very well to dry. Place turkey breast onto prepared rack.

6. Rub the turkey with the mustard, oil, and spices. Roast for 30 minutes. Lower temperature to 375°F; continue roasting for 45-50 minutes, until skin is golden and crisp.

7. Serve immediately or serve cold the next day.

OVEN-BAKED HONEY MUSTARD CHICKEN

This recipe has been making its rounds on my block. By now everyone serves it for dinner once a week, I'm sure. It's one of those dishes – you know, the classics – that fall under the categories:

Delicious.

Easy.

Kid proof.

Hubby proof.

Freezer proof.

What more can one ask? This one has made it into the supper rotation, no questions asked. It's a winner.

Thank you, Esty R., for sharing this recipe with me, the entire block, and now ... with all of you.

½ cup mayonnaise

½ cup plus 2 Tablespoons honey, *divided*

½ cup mustard

2 pounds chicken cutlets, *cut into nuggets*

2 cups cornflake crumbs

2 Tablespoons brown sugar

nonstick cooking spray

1. Preheat oven to 350°F. Place a mesh wire rack (such as a cookie cooling rack) onto a cookie sheet

2. In a small bowl, combine mayonnaise, ½ cup honey, and mustard. Add chicken. (At this point, you can marinate chicken in the fridge until ready to coat.)

3. In a shallow bowl, combine cornflake crumbs and brown sugar. Coat chicken cutlets in the crumb mixture. (Nuggets can be frozen at this point; defrost before baking.) Place coated nuggets onto prepared mesh wire rack. This will ensure the air circulates and renders a crispy well-baked nugget. Spray cutlets with nonstick spray. Drizzle remaining 2 tablespoons honey over the cutlets. Bake, uncovered, for 15-18 minutes.

MONDAY NIGHT'S CHICKEN SHISH-KEBABS

One of the best parts about writing recipes is that there's always dinner, even if mom was "working" all morning. Well, not always. I was testing some grilled meats one day, and knew my younger kids would not appreciate steak (especially the little one, who hasn't got that many teeth yet). So I threw on the grill some of our Monday Night's Chicken Shish-Kebabs, even if it was actually Wednesday.

Child D looked at me and asked with great seriousness, "It's Monday again?"

Then Child C, the youngest foodie I know, inquired "Are you including your Shish Kebabs in the book? I sure hope so. We all love them."

"Don't you think they are too plain?" I replied. Preparing them week in and week out, I guess, made them seem to me like regular, plain dinner.

"Plain? Look how pretty they look on the grill! All those colors! And people like easy recipes."

Keep in mind please that I was having this conversation with a 9-year-old.

"You might be right, you know," I replied. "I'll put them in." Hey, I thought, these are great. That's why we eat them every week.

1 (10-ounce) package pearl onions OR 1 regular onion, *cubed*

about 3 pounds chicken breast, *cubed into even chunks*

1 cup cherry tomatoes

½ red pepper, *cut into big squares*

½ orange pepper, *cut into big squares*

½ yellow pepper, *cut into big squares*

1 can whole button mushrooms, *drained*

5-6 mini zucchini, *sliced into 1 inch pieces,* OR 1 large zucchini, *not peeled, cubed*

½ cup oil

1 teaspoon salt (I like Lawry's seasoned salt here)

1 teaspoon paprika

1 teaspoon garlic powder

black pepper, *to taste*

SPECIAL EQUIPMENT
wooden or metal skewers

1. Place pearl onions into a bowl. Cover with boiling water; let sit for 5-10 minutes. Cut root end from each onion; squeeze at the other end to pop out onion.

2. Combine peeled onions with remaining ingredients in a large bowl. Cover; refrigerate (unless grilling within ½ hour). Marinate for ½ hour or up to 6 hours.

3. Let mixture rest at room temperature for at least ½ hour. Soak wooden skewers in water to prevent burning.

4. Turn gas grill to full heat, with the lid down. Thread chicken and vegetables onto skewers

5. Dip a folded paper towel into cooking oil, holding it with tongs. Wipe cooking grate carefully.

6. Place kebabs on grate; grill for about 4 minutes, until nice grill marks show. Using tongs, roll kebabs to other side. After a minute, turn heat to low. Close lid; grill for 8-10 minutes, depending on size of chicken chunks.

CANNOT BELIEVE THEY
ARE BAKED SPICY WINGS

My children wanted wings for dinner.

I was so lost. I've never even tasted wings, let alone cooked them. Wings are something that ends up in chicken stock, I thought. Wings cannot be eaten with a fork and knife without making a scene. Wings were not for me. I was convinced.

Like a good European mother trying to please her American children, I turned to my foodie friends and surrendered. Shushy Turin bailed me out with this amazing baked version, which, shockingly, is soooo good that I find myself sneaking a few while no one is looking.

Have plenty of napkins ready.

FOR THE WINGS

about 30 chicken wings

2 cups flour

1 teaspoon salt

½ teaspoon pepper

1 teaspoon paprika

½ teaspoon cumin

1 teaspoon garlic powder

FOR THE SAUCE

⅓ cup honey

¼ cup sriracha

¼ cup molasses

4 garlic cloves, *crushed*

2 Tablespoons teriyaki sauce

1. **Prepare the wings:** Mix the dry ingredients together in a bowl. Dredge the chicken wings in the bowl to coat with flour mixture. "Marinate" the chicken wings for at least 3 hours, covered, up to overnight, refrigerated.

2. Preheat oven to 375°F, or on roast setting, if possible.

3. Liberally drizzle a rimmed baking sheet with oil. Shake off coating from wings slightly; arrange wings on pan. Spray with nonstick cooking spray.

4. Bake for about 40 minutes, until golden and crispy.

5. **Prepare the sauce:** Toward the end of the cooking time, place honey and sriracha into a small pot; bring to a boil. Immediately reduce to a simmer; add molasses, garlic, and teriyaki. Stir well; keep warm until wings are baked.

6. Pour sauce over hot wings; toss to coat.

SNACKS
& SIDES

GAMES, SNACKS & A BIT OF NOSTALGIA...

Looking at a beautiful chessboard will forever give me nostalgia. So will the smell of roasting chestnuts.

I have made peace with the fact that there are certain things my kids will never fully understand about me. About my childhood, my upbringing, the places that made me who I am. Sure, I tell them all about it (and way too often, if you ask them). We even go back, for a visit, from time to time. But, still.

Certain things one can only experience, not explain.

When I was about 10 years old, my beloved grandfather decided it was time for me to learn how to play chess. Every Sunday, I would walk up the steep hill to my grandparents' apartment and sit for hours, deep in concentration. The game would take hours; each move was calculated. Zeidy didn't talk much during those winter afternoons. But I loved it. The quiet, the game, the quality time spent together. Already then, as a young girl, I knew: These Sundays were to be cherished, treasured. They were not a given.

Nonna would sometimes join us, with a tall glass of tea and a treat. Pistachios were my favorite. She would sit beside us and peel them for me with her elegant hands, placing the shelled ones alongside the chessboard. There were no interruptions, no phone calls, no doorbells. Just us, and the game.

I find myself thinking back, often, to those cozy moments. Life just got hectic after that. Like it always does.

Now I have my own family to gather around the table on cold winter nights. Homework is done, baths have been taken, teeth and hair have (hopefully) been brushed. What do you say to spending some quality time together with a good game? It doesn't have to be chess. Scrabble will do just fine, as long as we all gather around our table.

And as long as there is something delicious to munch on.

THE ART OF ROASTING CHESTNUTS

There is a man in Lugano who stands at the corner of Piazza Dante from October to February. His name is Giovanni; he's been selling chestnuts since the beginning of time (or at least so it seems). He's still roasting those same chestnuts, in those same roasters, then putting them in the same bags on the same scale. Just like when I was a kid. Nothing's changed but the price.

Buying chestnuts on the streets of any European town is as common as buying a bottle of soda in the U.S. It is part of the wintertime shopping experience; munching on that warm treat while warming your hands in the process.

The first time I saw chestnuts at the grocery store here in Lakewood, I have to admit, I did a little dance. As I was waiting in line to pay, I overheard two women discussing how to go about cooking those fruits. One was describing how she cooked them in water; the other woman claimed the microwave worked best. I hope my face didn't show my surprised look. I'd never heard of such thing. It occurred to me that most people here don't have a clue what chestnuts really taste like. I felt deeply saddened for them.

Well, today, I take the opportunity to give you the method that will bring out the true flavor of this amazing nut.

HOW TO PICK CHESTNUTS

Look for shiny, deep brown, healthy-looking chestnuts. When fresh, chestnuts will feel heavy for their size. Hold one between your fingers and press firmly. You don't want to feel the shell moving at all toward the flesh of the fruit. Also, check for small holes that may indicate worms.

HOW TO ROAST CHESTNUTS

1. Using a sharp knife, make an incision into the belly of each chestnut. Then cut another one over it, forming an "X." You want to go through the shell, just into the flesh.

2. Place chestnuts in one layer in a pot with holes at the bottom. (I use a pot-colander that came with a pasta pot. The bottom of my pot is visible in the photo.) Alternatively, you can use a disposable foil pan and use a knife to cut several holes into the bottom (but a pot is better).

3. Place pot over low heat so the flames reach the chestnuts through the holes. Swirl pot round and around from time to time. Roast for about 20 minutes, until chestnuts are slightly charred and shells are starting to pull away from fruit. You can also roast them in a 350°F oven for about 35 minutes, but the stovetop method is more genuine.

4. Peel while warm and experience the difference.

PRETZEL SAUSAGES

I was describing this recipe (while it was still an idea more than a recipe) to a friend. She seemed genuinely interested until I mentioned the word "dough." Or maybe it was the word "mixer." I forget. "Sounds fantastic, hon," she said, "but I ain't pulling out my mixer and getting all messy for a snack." That same night I gave it a try. My kids donned aprons and loved the idea of being part of a recipe in the making. It was easier than I had expected, even fun! Rolling out the dough was reminiscent of baking challah, but much simpler for those little hands, with no braiding required.

And the pretzels ... let's just say that they never actually made it to the table ....

I texted my above-mentioned friend a picture of the final product, and the prompt reply was, "You are putting me in such trouble. My son saw the pic. He's drooling. Am I gonna have to pull out my mixer?!?"

It's a good thing we live nearby. I just sent some over.

FOR THE DOUGH

1½ cups warm water

1 Tablespoon sugar

2¼ teaspoons active dry yeast

4½ cups flour

2 teaspoons salt

2 Tablespoons margarine, *melted and cooled*

FOR THE PRETZELS

about 7 cups water

½ cup baking soda

1 (12-ounce) package beef cocktail franks

1 large egg, *beaten*

sea salt, *for topping*

black pepper, *for topping*

1. In the bowl of a stand mixer fitted with the dough hook, combine warm water and sugar. Sprinkle in yeast; wait 10 minutes or so, until yeast starts activating.

2. Add flour, salt, and melted margarine. Mix on low speed until well combined. Increase speed to medium; knead until dough is smooth and pulls away from the side of the bowl. The dough will be a tad sticky. Place dough into a bowl (no need to grease bowl); cover tightly with plastic wrap. Let rise for about 1 hour.

3. Preheat oven to 425°F. Line 2 baking sheets with parchment paper; lightly brush paper with oil. In a large pot, over high heat, bring water and baking soda to a boil.

4. Meanwhile, pinch off golf ball-sized pieces of dough; form into thin, even strands. Wrap around hot dogs, making sure to secure the edges. (Hot dogs may be frozen at this point. Thaw before proceeding.)

5. Lower wrapped hot dogs, a few at a time, into the boiling water; boil for 30 seconds. Use a slotted spoon to transfer pretzels to prepared baking sheets. Brush pretzels with egg wash; sprinkle with salt and/or pepper.

6. Bake until deeply golden brown, 10-14 minutes. Serve warm with spicy brown mustard, if desired.

VIDEO TECHNIQUES

HOW TO ROLL SAUSAGES IN DOUGH AND PARBOIL THEM BEFORE BAKING

WWW.ARTSCROLL.COM/OURTABLEVIDEOS

SHEILA'S ARBES

Anyone related to Sheila knows that there's never a bad time to pop in and say hi. She will always greet you with a warm smile, fresh popcorn, and a tall glass of petel. But, if you can, try to stop by on an Erev Shabbos. That's when her legendary arbes make their appearance. And if you are lucky enough, you will also get a large "to go" bag which will most probably not make it back to your dira at all. They are that good.

NOTE

Sheila uses a pressure cooker to cook her *arbes*. If you own one, by all means use it. It will cut the cooking time in half. Because of the extended soaking time, the chickpeas won't bubble up as much as usual, so the vent won't be blocked by the foam.

1 pound dry chickpeas (garbanzo beans)

2 teaspoons salt

1 teaspoon black pepper

1 teaspoon sugar (or more), *to taste*

1. Place chickpeas into a large bowl of water, enough to cover by a good few inches (they will double in size and soak up the water, so give them enough water for that). Soak them for at least 24 hours, in a cool place (on the counter is fine, as long as it is 70-72 degrees in your kitchen). You can also freeze them after soaking (to save a step next time). I will typically start soaking them early Thursday morning and cook them on Friday.

2. Drain chickpeas; transfer to a large pot (or a pressure cooker; see Note). Cover with water; simmer in a covered pot, over low heat, until tender, about 4 hours. Make sure to keep an eye on the pot and give it a stir from time to time, adding water only if necessary. You will think that they are soft enough after 2 hours, but be patient. This is what makes them special: the super-soft texture.

3. Once chickpeas are soft, drain into a colander. Immediately spread them over a large, thick kitchen towel; let cool a bit.

4. Sprinkle chickpeas with salt, pepper, and sugar. Wring the towel so that excess water drains off and spices mix well. Taste and adjust seasoning to taste (some like it sweeter than others).

5. Serve warm.

See full-size photo on following page.

HOMEMADE EGG KICHEL

P || ABOUT 18 DOZEN

I had flown all the way to Switzerland, from one minute to the next, to pay a shivah visit to a close friend. Hours upon hours were spent sitting around, talking, sniffling, and eating. Yes, eating. There was this huge platter of homemade egg kichel that was so munch friendly, all we did was just dig for more and more. As I started seeing the bottom of the pan I made a mental note to request this recipe one day.

This recipe is a snap to prepare, no mixer necessary, no special equipment.

TIP

Cut your Kichel into any shape you like (I like long and narrow, like flatbreads). Then use them to plate your liver-and-eggs course with style.

3 eggs
½ cup oil
½ cup sugar
dash salt

½ teaspoon baking powder
2½ cups flour
sugar, cinnamon sugar, OR salt, *for sprinkling*

1. Preheat oven to 325°F. Prepare 3 baking sheets.

2. In a medium bowl, use a fork to combine eggs, oil, sugar, salt, baking powder, and flour. Knead until smooth.

3. Divide dough into 3 equal parts. Working with one at a time, roll out each between two sheets of parchment paper until dough covers entire area, to ensure uniformly thin kichlach. Gently peel off the top parchment paper; place dough, with bottom paper, to a baking sheet.

4. Using a sharp knife or fluted pastry cutter, score the dough into strips or diamond shapes; then sprinkle sugar, cinnamon sugar, or salt. Bake till golden (10-15 minutes) depending how well done you like them. Break apart at the score marks; store in an airtight container for up to a week.

See full-size photo on following page.

THE ISRAELI TAPENADE

P || 1½ CUPS

This dip is so delicious, most people ask me for the recipe after they taste it. One problem: It's not really a recipe. Is that a problem? Didn't think so.

My sister-in-law Rachel came up with this tapenade and we thank her every week. Does it say anywhere that salatim for Friday night need to be complicated to be delicious?

1 (19-ounce) can of pitted olives (I use the Israeli brands)

1 (19-ounce) can red pepper strips in vinegar (I use Bnei Darom brand)

1. Drain olives and hot peppers. Pulse in a food processor fitted with the "S" blade, until minced but still has some texture (see photo, page 147).

2. Refrigerate until ready to serve.

See full-size photo on following page.

FRIDAY NIGHT ROASTED GARLIC CONFIT

P || APPROX. ¾ CUP

This is what happens when you talk, style, and photograph food all day long; you learn new things. While working with great food photographers, I get tips and all kinds of fun tricks – like how to compose and light my iPhone photos better, and of course, new recipe ideas. This gem was a revelation by Hudi Greenberger, expert photographer and serious foodie.

Once you start serving these, warm, alongside your homemade, fresh, also warm, challah ... you'll see. There's no going back. Nuh uh. No going back.

Use the convenient pre-peeled garlic; it's a real timesaver. I have now solved the mystery of how one family alone can finish a Costco-size bag of pre-peeled garlic.

about 20 cloves garlic, *peeled*
good-quality olive oil (about ½ cup), *to cover*
dash freshly ground black pepper
dash sea salt
handful fresh herbs (I usually use rosemary and thyme); dry herbs will do well too, about a teaspoon (no, this is not an exact recipe)

1. Preheat oven to 350°F.

2. Place all ingredients into an ovenproof ramekin or small dish, making sure the olive oil covers the garlic. Bake, covered, for 45 minutes.

3. Remove from oven. Turn oven setting to broil. Pour mixture onto a larger baking pan. Broil for 10-15 minutes, watching closely. Stir from time to time, until slightly charred consistency is reached, but don't overdo it. The ideal texture is a bit toasted on the outside and spreadably soft on the inside.

4. Return roasted garlic and oil to the ramekin. Serve warm with challah.

NOTE

Garlic can be prepared a day in advance and refrigerated. Rewarm and serve. On Friday night, I usually place it on the hot plate to warm.

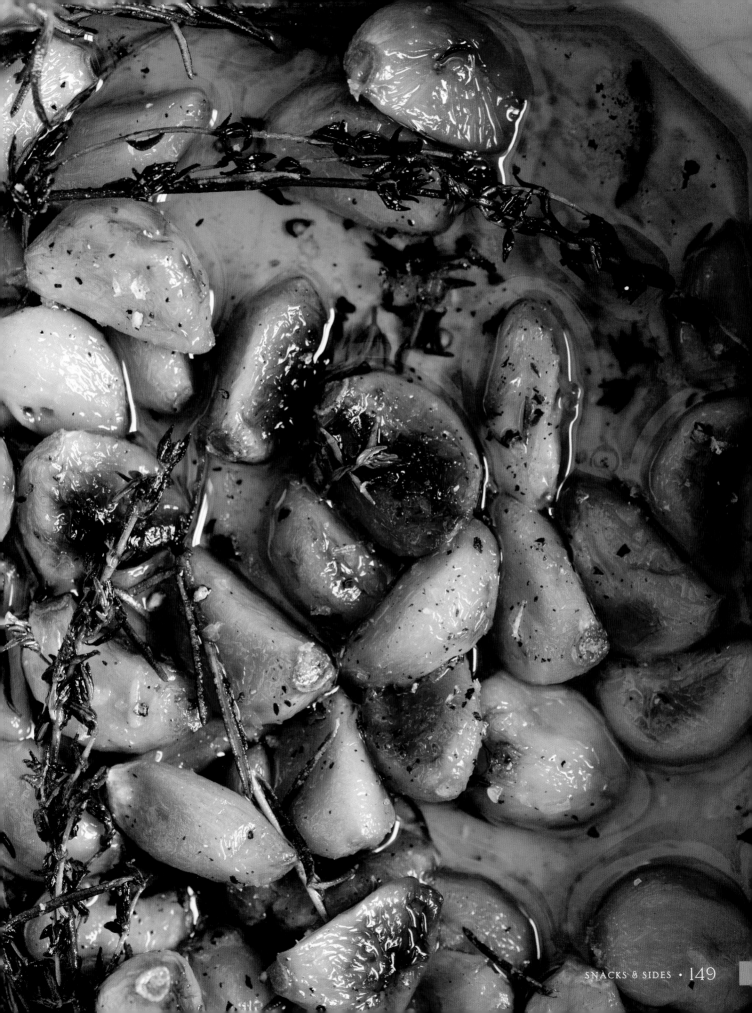

HOMEMADE POPCORN

In our home, we take popcorn very seriously. We would never settle for the microwaveable type. Never. Yes, we've had our fair share of smokin' kitchens and charred pots, but hey ... it's all worth it. We decided to take this hobby of ours to the next level one rainy Sunday, when no one was counting calories. That's how Caramel Popcorn was born; the caramel isn't too hard and is strangely compelling.

As for the Kettle Corn, the recipe takes us all the way to Hershey Park, Pennsylvania. Come Chol HaMoed Succos, the entire Muller clan packs off, every year, for a few days of fun with the cousins. My children await with great anticipation for this yearly family trip. But, in all honesty, all I anticipate is the park's legendary Kettle Corn. That's why I still agree to this yearly schlep.

You see, the park sells this amazing, fresh kosher-certified Kettle Corn. It's made on site, in these massive "pots," or better yet, kettles. The magic happens fast, and the aroma is incredible. We buy a bag as soon as we enter the park, and while the kids hit the rides, we, the adults, hit the popcorn.

This past Chol HaMoed, I struck up a conversation with the woman mixing the corn. I wasn't just being friendly, I was on a mission: I was determined to figure out how to prepare this treat in my own home. A few minutes of chitchat and unabashed flattery paid off really well. I had the formula.

As soon as my succah was down, I got to work. It wasn't easy. But a few bags of popcorn kernels later, I emerged victorious! I have a fantastic recipe – kettle corn in the comfort of my own home!

I also, ahem, have a few burned pots soaking in my garage. Sigh.

See full-size photo on following page.

KETTLE CORN

P || ABOUT 10 CUPS

⅓ cup oil

½ cup sugar

1 teaspoon salt, *divided*

½ cup popcorn kernels

1. Add oil to a heavy-bottomed 8-quart (or larger) pot; place over medium-high heat. Once oil starts warming up, add sugar, ½ teaspoon salt, and popcorn kernels. Stir mixture with a wooden spoon, until just combined. Cover.

2. Wearing oven mitts, shake pot. Return pot to heat. Do this repeatedly, 3 seconds of shaking the pot, and 3 seconds of returning the pot to the heat. Kernels will start popping. Keep alternating and shaking. Once popping slows down, remove popcorn from heat; carefully pour into a bowl. Add remaining salt; stir.

3. Store in an airtight container for up to a week.

CARAMEL POPCORN

nonstick cooking spray

3 Tablespoons oil

½ cup popcorn kernels

1½ teaspoons baking soda

3 cups sugar

1½ Tablespoons kosher salt

1½ ounces (3 Tablespoons)
  cold margarine, *cut into
  small pieces*

1 cup water

1. Spray two large heatproof spatulas and a large metal bowl with nonstick cooking spray.

2. **Prepare the popcorn:** Heat oil in a heavy-bottomed 8-quart (or larger) pot over high heat. Add popcorn kernels; cover pot, leaving it ajar. Shake pot back and forth; return to heat. Move the pot occasionally as the kernels pop. When popping slows almost to a stop, remove pot from heat (better a few unpopped kernels than burnt popcorn). Immediately pour popcorn into prepared bowl.

3. **Prepare the caramel:** Measure baking soda into a small dish. Line 2 baking sheets with parchment paper (or Silpats). In a 4-quart (or larger) pot, combine sugar, salt, margarine, and water. Gently stir with a spoon just to immerse the sugar. Using a pastry brush, brush down all sides of pot with water. Cook the sugar mixture over high heat WITHOUT STIRRING until it melts, bubbles, and turns a light golden caramel color on top; this will take 10-20 minutes, depending on your stove. Watch closely, as the color change happens fast. Remove pot from heat.

4. Place pot on a safe surface (or into the sink) in case the caramel spills over. Working quickly, stir in baking soda. Caramel will bubble up. The baking soda aerates the caramel, which makes it easier to eat when it cools but causes it to bubble vigorously now, so be careful.

5. Immediately pour bubbling caramel over the popcorn. Don't scrape out the pot; just use what pours out easily. Immediately use the spatulas to toss the popcorn in the caramel. Pour coated popcorn onto prepared baking sheets; use the spatulas to pat it into one flat layer.

6. When it is cool enough to touch, use your hands to break the layer into small clusters. Cool completely; store in an airtight container for up to 1 week.

SEA SALT CARAMELS

I had a good laugh when I sat down to re-write this popular recipe from my very first column in Ami. The intro read:

"No, this is not a typo. This is candy with salt on top."

It was February of 2012. Putting salt onto sweet caramel was something seriously odd.

Fast forward to 2016. Salted Caramel is so everywhere, we practically are about to put it into a sushi roll.

Is it going out of style? Not a chance. Salty and sweet is such a winning combination that it never gets old.

These caramels are one of those things that I remember I have in the refrigerator (hidden, of course, behind the huge Costco-size grape juice) on a rainy day, and smile to myself, knowing something delicious awaits. No words that I can write here will convince you about them more than tasting one yourself.

My family members all have different ways of eating them. Child A loves to keep them in the freezer so that they slowly thaw on her tongue (that's what she told me, but you and I both know that the freezer is the perfect place to hide items you don't want your little caramel-obsessed brother – aka Child C – to find). Child B likes to keep them at room temperature even though that might result in a sticky wrapper ("That's what teeth are for," he quipped). Child C claims he will eat them any way as long as I make a huge batch ("There's never enough! Child A hides them all!" He has a point), and finally Child D said she liked the apple ones better because salt doesn't belong on a candy (somebody tell her it's 2016, please.) I personally prefer them stored in the refrigerator and savored, slowly, with a cup of coffee.

Check out the video simply to see how quickly, easily, and with few basic ingredients, caramels can happen in your own home. Many people are intimidated by homemade candy. Mention a thermometer and they will break into a sweat. But watch the video, gain some confidence, get into the mood, and then, pull out a pot. It's really simple.

1½ cups sugar

¼ cup water

¼ cup light corn syrup

5 Tablespoons butter

1 cup heavy cream

1 heaping teaspoon sea salt

½ teaspoon pure vanilla extract

finishing salt, such as Maldon Sea Salt Flakes or Fleur de Sel (may substitute with coarse sea salt)

VIDEO TECHNIQUES

HOW TO COOK CARAMELS; HOW TO CUT AND WRAP THE CANDY

WWW.ARTSCROLL.COM/OURTABLEVIDEOS

1. Line an 8-inch loaf pan with parchment paper, allowing it to drape over two long sides; brush the paper lightly with oil. Set aside.

2. In a heavy, deep saucepan (at least 5 inches deep) combine sugar, water, and corn syrup. Bring to a boil over medium-high heat. Boil until the mixture is a warm golden brown. Don't stir — just swirl the pan. Watch carefully, it will go from golden to dark rather quickly.

3. Meanwhile, in a second pot, melt together butter, heavy cream, and salt. Bring to a simmer (do not boil); turn off heat. Set aside.

4. When the sugar mixture is golden brown, turn off heat and slowly add the cream mixture to the sugar mixture. Careful! It will bubble up violently! Use a wooden spoon to stir in the vanilla; return to heat. Stirring from time to time, cook over medium-low

heat for 5-7 minutes, until the mixture reaches 248°F on a candy thermometer. (I strongly recommend the use of a candy thermometer. It's an inexpensive tool that will take out all the guesswork. However, if you do not own one, watch the caramel closely and test it by dropping some onto a dish. You will know it's ready when it holds its shape and does not run when tilted. But again, a candy thermometer will ensure a perfect candy and no doubt. If you leave the caramel cooking for too long, it will result in a tough candy, hard to chew.)

5. When caramel reaches 248°F, carefully pour caramel into the prepared pan; refrigerate for a few hours, until firm.

6. Remove caramel from pan; peel off parchment paper. Place caramel on a cutting board; sprinkle with finishing salt. Gently press salt into caramel. Cut into strips, then into even pieces. (It's easier to cut the caramels if you brush the knife with a flavorless oil.)

7. Cut parchment paper into 4 x 5-inch rectangles. Wrap each candy individually in the cut papers, twisting the ends (see photo below). Store in an airtight container in the refrigerator.

See full-size photos on following page.

MAKE AHEAD

Caramels will stay fresh in the fridge for at least 10 days. Caramels freeze well. Recipe doubles well.

TIP

Pour some caramel into a mason jar. Refrigerate. Rewarm in the microwave for a few seconds and serve over ice cream or cake, for a delightful treat.

NOTE

What are finishing salts? Enter any upscale grocery and you will find a variety of different, colorful, and exciting salts. While mostly relying on my favorite, the kosher salt, I do own a variety of salts with which I like to experiment. I've found that Himalayan Pink Salt goes really well with red meat (and they even sell it in Costco!). Maldon Sea Salt is my new favorite, due to its crunchy texture and delicate flakiness. I often snack on it, straight out of the box ... it works well on edamame or simple sliced crudités, such as tomatoes and radishes. I prefer it for my caramels. Fleur de Sel is very refined and also commonly used for caramels and other candies.

All specialty salts can be found online, and today, in many groceries.

GRANNY SWEETS

Have you looked at these apples? Would you believe me if I told you they taste as good as they look?

These apples have been my staple mishloach manos for the last four years, along with the Irresistible Toffee (page 170). Rumor has it that some husbands or children never get to see these apples because some wives or mothers conveniently "misplace" them as soon as they receive them. One friend said she cuts the apple into seven pieces – to last her all week.

The following year I sent her seven apples. It was a true chessed.

Choose pretty apples that stand upright on their own. I was so engrossed the other day at the farmers market, picking my precious apples one by one, resting them on the palm of my hand and looking at them from all angles. That is, until I noticed the guy unloading the fruit looking at me with such pity in his eyes.

8 medium Granny Smith apples

1 recipe Sea Salt Caramels (page 154), *Steps 2-4*

CHOICE OF TOPPINGS

1 cup shelled pistachios

1 cup roasted salted sunflower seeds

1 cup shelled pumpkin seeds

72% cacao bittersweet chocolate

EQUIPMENT

8 lollipop or popsicle sticks, *optional* (You can also just use the stem of the apple.)

VIDEO TECHNIQUES

HOW TO DIP APPLES IN PREPARED CARAMEL; HOW TO TOP APPLES WITH NUTS

WWW.ARTSCROLL.COM/OURTABLEVIDEOS

1. Scrub apples, one by one, under hot soapy water. Rinse well. This step is crucial to ensure you remove all wax from the apples, otherwise the caramel will slide right off. If using lollipop sticks, remove stems. Insert stick into the core, making sure it is well secured. Place apples into freezer for at least 20 minutes.

2. **Prepare the toppings:** Place shelled pistachios, if using, into a resealable plastic bag. Crush nuts with the bottom of a glass bottle or with a meat mallet. Set aside. Place each topping of your choice onto a disposable plate. Place chocolate, if using, into a microwaveable bowl; melt chocolate in microwave. Set aside.

3. Line a baking sheet with parchment paper. Grease the parchment paper; set aside.

4. Prepare steps 2 through 4 of the Sea Salt Caramels.

5. Turn off heat and let temperature of caramel drop from 248°F to 200°F. This will happen rather quickly. Stir caramel from time to time. Remove apples from the freezer. One by one, immerse in the caramel. Lift apple out of the caramel; let the excess drip back into the pot. Roll apple in the prepared toppings; press them in with your hand, if necessary. Place the apple, stick-side up, onto the prepared cookie sheet. Refrigerate. For caramel-and-chocolate-dipped apples: Dip apple in caramel first. Refrigerate for a few minutes. Dip into melted chocolate, then into toppings. Refrigerate.

6. If the caramel starts to harden and becomes difficult to work with, return to heat and reheat caramel to desired consistency.

7. Remove apples from refrigerator a half-hour before serving or slicing. Caramel apples will stay fresh for a week in the refrigerator, 3-4 days at room temperature.

See full-size photo on following page.

ENERGY BALLS

Karen, mom to three energetic, always on-the-go teens, introduced me to this fabulous recipe. She keeps these in her freezer for a quick "pick me up" or as a snack for the kids. Either way, they're pure energy, the natural way. And so delicious, too.

And my kids still have no clue that these treats are good for them.

Shhhhh. Don't tell.

While very healthy, the balls are not dietetic, so don't start popping a ton of them. But they're a great solution for when you need a treat.

NOTE _____

This recipe is very flexible. If you choose to omit one ingredient you can easily double any of the other ingredients. Also, if you don't want to use the PB2, which is a powder made from peanuts, you can substitute with any jar of nut butter, whether peanut, cashew, almond ... although I do recommend the PB2 for its lower fat content.

1 (6.5 ounce) jar PB2 (regular or chocolate flavor)

½ jar of water (use the PB2 jar)

¼ cup steel cut oats

½ cup old-fashioned rolled oats

¼ cup wheat germ

¼ cup chia seeds

¼ cup sunflower seeds, *plus more for coating, optional*

¼ cup coconut flakes, *plus more for coating, optional*

¼ cup mini chocolate chips (sugar-free), *plus more for coating, optional*

¼ cup flax seeds, *plus more for coating, optional*

¼ cup raisins, *plus more for coating, optional*

¼ cup cocoa powder, *plus more for coating, optional*

1. Combine PB2 and water to form a paste. Add remaining ingredients and mix well with your hands.

2. Roll into walnut-size balls. Roll balls into any of the coating components of your choice, or leave plain. Freeze.

3. Let thaw for a few minutes before serving.

CHOCOLATE CRANBERRY GRANOLA

I really wanted to call this "The Incredible Chocolate Cranberry Granola, Infused with Silan." But it didn't fit on the page quite as neatly as I wished.

TIP _____

I like to keep a mason jar (or two) of this granola in the freezer at all times. I find this works well when hosting an impromptu breakfast or *shalosh seudos*. All you'll need to do is buy some yogurt, cut up some fruit, and voila ... you have a yogurt bar where your guests can create their own parfaits: filling, beautiful, and nourishing.

3 cups old-fashioned rolled oats

1 cup steel cut oats

¾ cup wheat germ

¾ cup oat bran

1 cup roasted salted sunflower seeds

1 cup slivered almonds

1 cup chopped walnuts

¾ teaspoon salt

¼ cup brown sugar

¼ cup honey

¼ cup oil

¼ cup silan (date honey)

2 teaspoons cinnamon

2 teaspoons pure vanilla extract

1 cup chocolate chips

1 cup dried cranberries

1. Preheat oven to 325°F. Line a baking sheet with parchment paper; set aside.

2. In a large bowl, combine all oats, wheat germ, oat bran, sunflower seeds, almonds, and walnuts.

3. In a small saucepan, over low heat, stir together salt, brown sugar, honey, oil, silan, cinnamon, and vanilla extract. Bring to a gentle simmer, constantly stirring. Pour mixture over the dry ingredients; stir to coat. Spread mixture in an even layer on the baking sheet.

4. Bake for 20 minutes, stirring once halfway. Mixture will be soft and gooey, but do not bake longer than directed. Granola will harden as it cools. Remove granola from the oven; immediately stir in chocolate chips and cranberries. The chocolate will melt, coating the granola and forming clumps here and there. Once cooled, transfer granola to an airtight container. Granola will stay fresh for 2-3 weeks.

HONEY WALNUT BRITTLE

I literally grew up munching on these treats. You know how some flavors take you back to your childhood? This does it for me.

You have to understand the whole picture. Lugano had almost no kosher candy in my days. Sure, we had chips, pretzels, and lots of Swiss chocolate. But that was pretty much it. Every Purim, Mrs. Weiss would send this insanely delicious homemade brittle. My siblings and I always fought over who got "the bigger piece."

My mother prepares this as a Pesach snack, too. I called for the recipe and prepared batch #1. It was Thursday; we were shooting pix on Tuesday. Brittle holds up, right? Wrong! THIS brittle is eaten very fast by little (or large) pantry thieves who officially brushed their teeth already. ("Ma!! This is sooo good!! Make more! I didn't get as much as he did." Why does that sound so familiar??). So "Ma" made more. Batch #2. And then hid it really well. Or so she thought.

Let's just say that saving some for the photo entailed some very creative thinking. And batch #4.

Now whenever I brag that I grew up with no junk food ... no food coloring, only organic, unprocessed foods ... they cut me short and say, "But Ma, you had honey walnut brittle. That's wayyyy better than junk."

Hmmmmm. Touché.

1 (6-ounce) bag walnut nibs
(walnuts chopped small)

½ cup honey

1½ Tablespoons sugar

1. Preheat oven to 350°F. Line a baking sheet with parchment paper. Spray parchment paper with nonstick cooking spray.

2. Spread the walnut nibs on a second baking sheet. Toast the walnut nibs for 5 minutes.

3. In a heavy-bottomed saucepan, combine honey and sugar. Bring to a simmer, stirring from time to time.

4. Carefully add the nuts to the honey. Stir to combine; continue cooking over low heat, stirring continuously, for about 10 minutes, until mixture starts to brown at the sides of the saucepan and begins to thicken. You may think brittle is burning, but don't worry; you're looking for that darker, thicker consistency. Immediately pour onto the prepared baking sheet and spread as quickly as possible (it will harden fast). Allow to cool.

5. Once cooled, break brittle into wedges, and then hide in an airtight box. Don't worry about shelf life, they will not last.

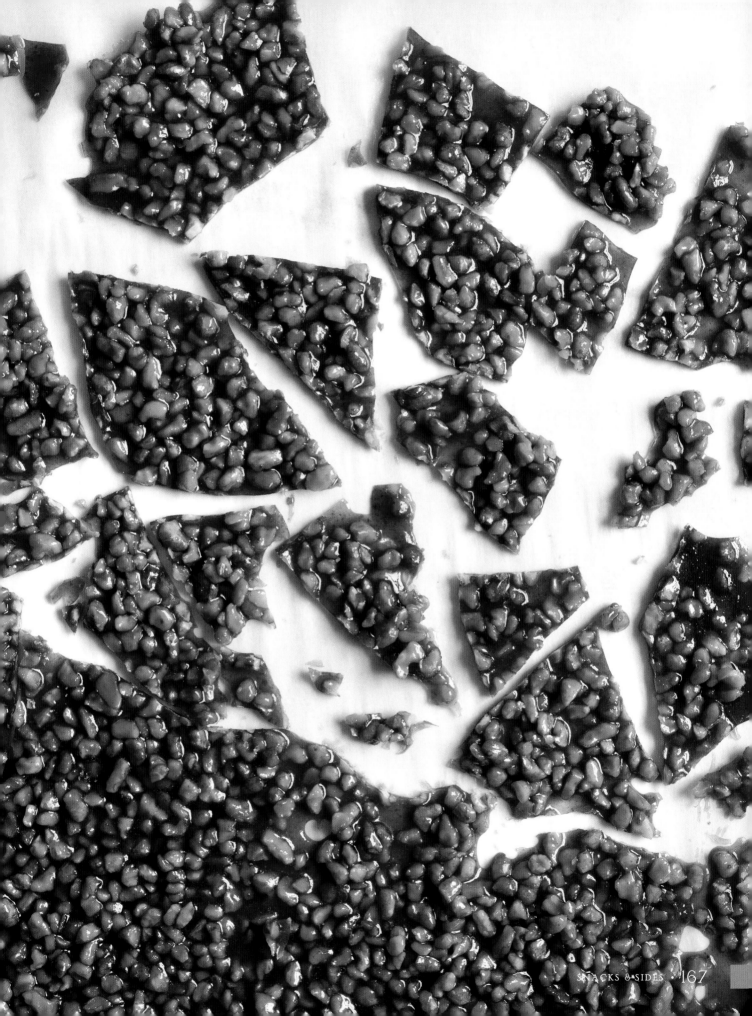

HEALTHY GRANOLA BARS

Do you also have those days when you search for something to grab on the run, something you can eat at a red light while on hold with Dr. Shanik's office and passing tissues to the back seat?

What, I am the only one with these mornings?

I didn't think so ....

We all need these lifesavers. Something that's filling yet healthy. Something that won't give you a sugar crash 20 minutes later. Something that won't kill your diet.

And, most importantly, something delicious.

Well, great news everyone: Here it is.

TIP

I like to pop these granola bars into individual resealable bags (the snack-size bags work well) and then freeze them. This way it's literally a "grab and go" snack, for kids and adults alike.

Oh, and one more thing. Child A likes them microwaved, warm and gooey. Child B eats them frozen, straight up. I, on the other hand, like to dip one into a cup of milk. To each his own.

2 cups old-fashioned rolled oats

1 cup steel cut oats

½ cup flax seeds

1 cup whole spelt

1 cup coarsely chopped pecans

½ cup roasted salted sunflower seeds

½ teaspoon kosher salt

2 teaspoons cinnamon

¼ cup oil

½ cup honey

1 cup applesauce

2 teaspoons pure vanilla extract

1 cup chocolate chips, *optional*

1. Line a 9 x 13-inch pan with parchment paper. Preheat oven to 350°F.

2. In a large skillet, toast all oats over medium heat. Keep stirring until oats are golden and fragrant, 10-15 minutes. Set aside to cool.

3. In a large bowl, combine remaining dry ingredients. Add cooled oats. Using a spatula, stir in oil, honey, applesauce, and vanilla. If using, add chocolate chips at this point.

4. Press into prepared pan. Bake for 35-40 minutes. Cool completely.

5. Once cooled, use a sharp serrated knife to cut into bars. Store in an airtight container or freeze. Bars will stay fresh in an airtight container for a few days, but it's best to freeze them.

IRRESISTIBLE TOFFEE

When you have to hide something from yourself, deep inside the freezer, and pretend that it's not there, you know you are in trouble.

This toffee lives up to its name. It's not something you want to have lying around if you are trying to watch your waistline. No amount of self-control will get you past this temptation. You'll need to trust me on this.

If you happen to know me, you'll definitely recognize this candy. It's the one that I've been sending for mishloach manos for years now. Actually, one Purim, I changed things around a bit

and sent basil-infused olives and chatzilim instead. It worked with my Yerushalmi theme. But, nobody cared about the Yerushalmi theme. They wanted the toffee. People were waaaaaaiting for toffee, staying milchigs for it, even.

Neighbors were disappointed. Friendships tested.

I hate disappointing people. So we are back with the toffee. Every. Single. Purim.

And year round too.

Thank you, Z.L., for this incredible recipe.

---

2 sticks (1 cup) butter, *cut into pieces*

1½ cups sugar

2 Tablespoons water

1 Tablespoon light corn syrup

1 cup chopped pecans

16 ounces bittersweet chocolate, *chopped, divided*

½ cup shelled pistachios, *chopped*

1 (3.5-ounce) bar good-quality white chocolate (I use Choco Blanc), *chopped*

nonstick cooking spray

1. Line a baking sheet with parchment paper, covering the sides, too. Set aside.

2. In a medium saucepan over medium heat, combine butter, sugar, water, and corn syrup. Mix with a wooden spoon from time to time, until butter melts. Once butter has melted, increase heat to medium-high and insert a candy thermometer.

3. Cook mixture until golden brown and registering 300°F on candy thermometer, about 10 minutes. Do not stir. (I strongly recommend the use of a candy thermometer. However, if you do not own one, you can tell when the toffee is ready by its color. Wait for it to turn a warm beige.)

4. Remove saucepan from heat; carefully stir in the chopped pecans.

5. Quickly pour toffee onto prepared baking pan. Spread to the edges, using a spatula, working quickly to prevent hardening. Let stand for 30 minutes.

6. Melt half the bittersweet chocolate (see Note); spread over cooled toffee. Refrigerate until firm, about 30 minutes.

7. Once firm, flip entire bar over and peel off the parchment paper. Let toffee come to room temperature for 5 minutes or so. (This will help you with the next step and prevent chocolate from hardening too quickly.)

8. Melt the remaining bittersweet chocolate. Spread over toffee bar; immediately sprinkle with pistachios. (Once chocolate hardens, pistachios won't stick.)

9. Melt white chocolate (see Note). Cool a bit; then pour into a resealable plastic bag. Snip off a corner of the bag; drizzle white chocolate over the entire bar and pistachios. Freeze until firm.

10. Once chocolate is firm, break bar into bite-sized pieces. Store in an airtight container at room temperature or in the freezer. Toffee will stay fresh for about a month at room temperature.

See full-size photos on following page.

NOTE

I own a dairy microwave exclusively for melting chocolate. I'm not kidding. When melting regular bittersweet chocolate, start by chopping the bar into chunks then microwaving for 1 minute. Give it a quick stir; then return to the microwave for another 30 seconds. Stir again, and, only if necessary, return for another 30 seconds.

White chocolate is more delicate and can scorch easily. It's best to chop the white chocolate into very small, even pieces before microwaving. Start with 30 seconds, then melt at 15-second intervals, stirring between each. Microwave the chocolate for as short a time as possible. Stir vigorously to get to get the chocolate smooth rather than returning it to the microwave again.

This recipe is best stored in the refrigerator, but it's not a must — a cool dry place will do as well. It also doubles, triples, and even quadruples well (!). Yep, I've made my fair share of toffee ....

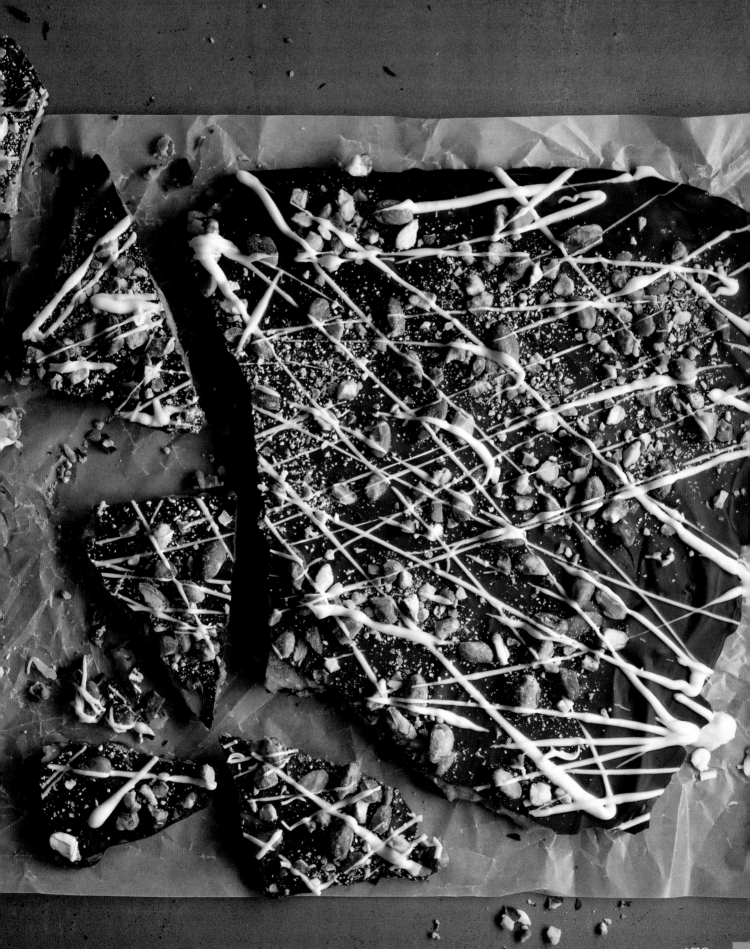

PAIN AÚ CHOCOLAT

Pain aú Chocolat, as you probably guessed already, means chocolate bread. And that's all it is, dough and chocolate. Deliciously simple and so satisfying. The almost-salty puff pastry complements the sweet chocolate. Best of all, with only three ingredients, it is quickly assembled and easily enjoyed ... and always a hit, no matter at what age.

Traditionally, pain aú chocolat is made with chocolate sticks. That's how we bake them in Europe, but I still haven't met any pareve chocolate sticks in the US. I find that a row of a regular chocolate bar works just as well.

10 (5 x 5-inch) puff pastry squares

2 (3.5 ounce) 72% dark chocolate bars (I use Schmerling's)

1 egg, *lightly beaten, for egg wash*

1. Preheat oven to 375°F. Line a baking sheet with parchment paper; set aside.

2. Cut chocolate into rows of 4 cubes each (6 strips per bar).

3. Place a row of chocolate onto a pastry square; fold dough over to cover the chocolate. Place each pastry, seam side down, onto the baking sheet. Repeat with remaining chocolate and pastry squares.

4. Brush pastries with egg wash; bake until golden, 25-30 minutes. Serve immediately.

BREADS, CAKES & COOKIES

TO BE A CHILD

My daughter wakes up at 5:25 a.m. today. Way too early. Too early, even if mom had gone to bed at a decent hour. "I'm starving," she declares.

"Go to the kitchen, there's a surprise for you on the counter," I tell her, one eye open.

She's gone in a flash. Twenty seconds later: Pitter-patter. She's back.

"Where's the confekshuhn sugar??"

Of course. I forgot the most important part. I tell her where to find it. Pitter-patter. Screeeech. Chair being dragged to the counter. Cabinet opens. Slam. Cabinet closes. And finally, some quiet. I drift into blissful sleep. The next thing I know, I have a 5-year-old covered in confectioners' sugar snuggling next to me.

"Ma? Is it Shavuos today?"

"No, dear."

"Tomorrow??"

"No, Shavuos will come in about three weeks."

"Ma?"

"Yes, sweetie."

"Thank you for baking Kaas Potjes even if it's not really Shavuos."

My kitchen has seasons, just like the weather. Your kitchen has seasons too, I'm sure.

On Erev Rosh Hashanah, we bake honey muffins and round, fluffy challos. Succos is reserved for specialties we don't indulge in year round, like gooey babka. Chanukah spells latkes, funnel cakes, and batter-fried chicken. Purim brings lots of goodies that aren't usually allowed. And Caramel Apples, of course. You can tell it's Pesach when Fudge Bombs and Almond Chews are consumed in large quantities. Oh, don't forget the beloved egg "lukshen." And Shavuos is cheese. Cheese cakes, cheese pots, cheese everything. I love it when my children recognize the seasons according to what is cooking. I know I am giving them the aromas that every childhood deserves.

It's my turn to form the sweet memories all of us have: Those of our mamas lovingly preparing our favorite dishes for every chag, creating a legacy for years to come. I take immense pride in giving my children those memories, those moments in the kitchen, when we are elbow deep in batter or laughing over a flopped icing. I know the mess will be cleaned up ... eventually. But the memories ... those will be etched forever.

RENEE'S CHALLAH NOTES

"The challah makes your Shabbos table," says my zia (aunt, in Italian), full of passion. "The moment when you remove the challah cover and the shiny braided homemade challah is revealed, that's when I swell with pride. There's nothing like a homemade challah to complete your Shabbos table. It's the fruit of a woman's hard work, lovingly kneading, patiently braiding. It's our mitzvah, and I cherish it every time I put up a batch of dough."

I had the honor of spending a delightful afternoon in the company of my zia. We laughed, we reminisced, and we philosophized. We also baked challah. Her expert hands moved quickly, knowingly, braiding perfect challos in no time. All I did was watch in awe.

Zia started baking when she was 14 years old and has never stopped. Her challos are legendary in Yerushalayim. I learned quite a few things on that cozy afternoon in February.

• It is imperative to use lukewarm water to activate the yeast (110-115°F). If your water is too hot it will "kill" the yeast. Wait for yeast to activate. If, after 10 minutes or so, your yeast does not start bubbling and foaming a bit, discard it and start over. Your yeast might have been too old or the water too hot/cold.

• For the whole wheat recipe, I like to use a combination of white whole wheat and spelt flours. I found this blend results in the lightest and softest challah. But I have made this recipe with whole wheat only, spelt only, and white whole wheat only. They were all great, and all different. Feel free to experiment to your liking.

• Salt could "kill" yeast, too. When placing the salt into the flour, dig a little hole in the flour, spoon the salt into it, and then cover the salt with flour.

• Here's a neat trick: Measure the oil first and swirl it around a bit in the measuring cup while pouring. Measure the honey next. Your honey will glide right out of your pre-greased measuring cup.

• I like to knead the dough for a good 10 minutes. Once those 10 minutes are up, I turn off the machine, count to 20 (exactly the time needed to line a large bowl with a plastic bag and spray the inside of the bag with nonstick cooking spray — see the next note if you are raising your eyebrows in wonder), and then run the machine again, for 5-10 seconds longer. This is a little trick I learned along the way from one of the many challah gurus out there. It helps stabilize the dough gluten so that your challos won't "blow up" in the oven and fall apart all over the place. (Ever had that happen? It's so upsetting!!)

• I find that the best place for the dough to rise is inside a large, food-safe plastic bag. Yup, you heard me. Line a large bowl or box with a big plastic bag, spray the inside with cooking spray, and place dough inside. Fold over top of bag, cover with a blanket or large towel, and let rest. The plastic creates the perfect hot and humid environment for the dough to rise. And read between the lines: no bowl to wash! I know you will try it, just for that alone.

• To achieve beautiful, even loaves, it is important to focus on the strands. First, you want to make sure they are even in size. Zia recommended weighing them, and as soon I started I was hooked. It makes all the difference. I find 4.5-5 ounces per strand works for me. Second, roll those strands to perfection. You want to see a gradual increase toward the middle, not a big belly.

• For an extra shine, brush with egg wash, let stand for 15 minutes, and then brush again. You may need another lightly beaten egg for the wash.

• The oatmeal on top of the whole wheat challah is optional, but I highly recommend it for a few reasons:

  ▪ It gives the challah a beautiful, earthy look.

  ▪ It will help you differentiate between the whole wheat challos and the regular ones, once they are frozen.

  ▪ It tastes great. Crunchy, chewy, delicious.

• Freeze challos, unless you will use them that same day.

• Rewarm challos briefly in the oven before serving.

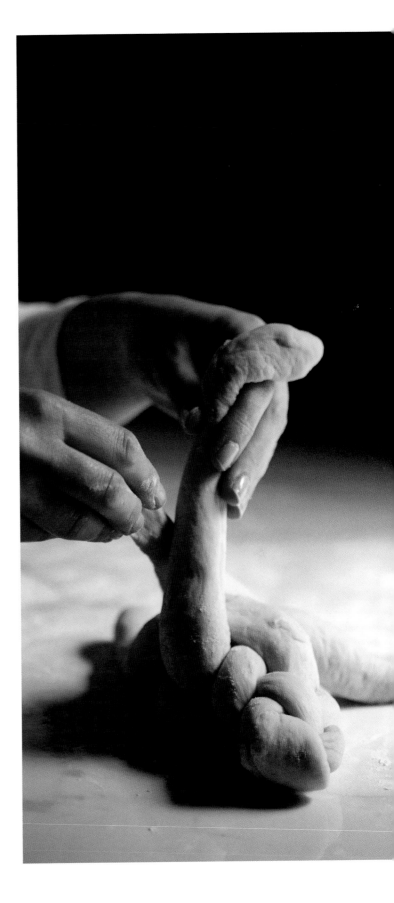

MY MOST FAVORITE WHITE FLOUR CHALLAH

Do you own a folder where you keep all your favorite recipes? I'm sure you do. In my folder you will find this old, stained index card entitled "Ayala's Challah." I periodically reorganize my folder and rewrite recipes, but I will never do that with this one. It is about 15 years old and has lots of charm. On the back, there is a list: broom, shovel, drying rack, iron, colander, laundry basket .... Yes, we were newlyweds; among the things we needed to start a home was a great challah recipe.

I've been baking it ever since, referring back to that stained card and never changing a thing. Every Shabbos, on our table, you will find one whole wheat challah and one white flour challah. Shabbos without homemade challah just isn't the same.

I really love this challah. It has great texture and taste. It's not too "eggy" and not too soft. There's enough crust for the adults, yet a fluffy center for the kids. The dough is a pleasure to work with. I seldom flour my counter when braiding. And the mixer bowl has almost nothing left in it when I am done. I can mix the whole wheat dough next, without washing the bowl first.

In the video tutorial, you'll see that I bake my challos on lined baking sheets. Of course, you can bake them in pans. I just like the traditional challah look better.

---

3 ounces fresh yeast OR ¼ cup minus ½ teaspoon active dry yeast

¾ cup plus 1 Tablespoon sugar, *divided*

1 cup warm water (110-115°F)

5 pounds flour

3 Tablespoons kosher salt

½ cup oil

3 eggs

2 egg yolks

3¼ cups water

coarsely ground cornmeal, *optional*

1 egg, *lightly beaten, for egg wash*

VIDEO TECHNIQUES

HOW TO BRAID CHALLAH FROM 4 STRANDS OF DOUGH; HOW TO FORM ROUND CHALLOS

WWW.ARTSCROLL.COM/OURTABLEVIDEOS

1. Place yeast, 1 tablespoon sugar and warm water into a medium bowl. Let yeast activate, 10-15 minutes (see Challah Notes, page 180).

2. Meanwhile, place flour (no need to sift, not for texture) and remaining sugar into the bowl of a stand mixer fitted with the dough hook. Give it one quick whirl, just to combine. Dig a little hole in the flour. Spoon the salt into the hole; cover with flour.

3. Add oil, eggs, and egg yolks; then add the activated yeast, followed by the water. Mix on low until dough forms, then on high for at least 10 minutes. Dough should be elastic and not stick to the sides of the bowl. (If it does stick, add 1 tablespoon of flour at a time until the desired consistency is reached.)

4. Line a large bowl with a large food-safe plastic bag. Spray the inside of the bag with cooking spray; place the dough into the bag. Fold over top of bag (but don't tie it shut); cover with a heavy blanket or towel. I use a down cover. Let the dough rest for 1 hour. After 1 hour, punch the dough down a bit; let rest for another ½ hour.

5. Preheat oven to 400°F.

6. Line 2 baking sheets with parchment paper. Sprinkle liberally with cornmeal (if using); set aside. Alternatively, use challah pans. Make sure you grease them well with oil or cooking spray.

7. Divide the dough into 4 or 6 equal parts. Work with one part at a time. Divide dough, depending on how many strands you wish to braid. (Check out our video to see how to form strands and braid challah.) Shape each part into a strand. Braid strands to form the challah shape; place onto the prepared baking sheets or into challah pan. Repeat with remaining dough. Cover with a towel; let rise 10 minutes-1 hour. (I personally don't like to let the challos rise too long here; I allow only 20 minutes. There is an ongoing family dispute that claims a longer second rise is extremely important.)

8. Use a pastry brush to coat challos with egg wash, covering all sides.

9. Place the challos into the preheated oven. Bake for 10 minutes; lower the temperature to 350°F and bake for additional 25-30 minutes (depending on size of challos).

10. Remove challos from oven and turn upside down on towels to cool.

NOTE _____

I don't usually bake challos on a Friday. When I do bake them, I double wrap them in plastic bags and freeze. Before Shabbos, I place them in the oven at 200°F (no need to defrost prior) and leave them there until the *seudah*. We are big fans of warm challah. On Shabbos day, I place my challos on top of the cholent to warm up.

See full-size photo on following page.

REALLY, REALLY GOOD WHOLE WHEAT CHALLAH

I was always convinced that whole wheat bread was something I would eventually learn to like. Probably around the time I was going to turn 60.

But was I wrong. It happened way before that.

I first tasted this delicious challah about 14 years back, at my cousin's house. I was so amazed by how good it was, I refused to believe it was actually whole wheat. Everyone, and I mean EVERYONE (aka men and children), at the table was eating it so happily, leaving the white flour one untouched. That same week I called her for that precious recipe, and I've been baking it ever since.

TIP

You may add water to the seltzer, if necessary, to reach 4½ cups.

NOTE

Because of its high yeast content, the dough should not rise for more than 40 minutes to prevent an overly yeasty flavor.

---

6 ounces fresh yeast OR ½ cup minus 1 Tablespoon active dry yeast

4 Tablespoons sugar (preferably organic)

1 liter (1 bottle) seltzer (4½ cups), *divided*

8 cups whole wheat flour (I use white whole wheat)

8 cups whole spelt flour

3½ Tablespoons kosher salt

½ cup oil

1 cup honey

4 eggs

½ cup cornmeal, *optional*

2 eggs, *lightly beaten, for egg wash*

½ cup old-fashioned rolled oats, *optional*

---

1. Place yeast and sugar into a medium bowl. Warm to lukewarm in microwave for 1 minute (see Challah Notes, page 180). Pour 2 cups seltzer over yeast and sugar. Let yeast activate, 10 minutes or so.

2. Meanwhile, place flours, salt (see Challah Notes), oil, honey, and eggs into the bowl of a stand mixer fitted with the dough hook. Heat remaining 2½ cups seltzer in microwave for 1 minute. Add yeast mixture and seltzer to bowl. Knead dough for 5-7 minutes.

3. Transfer dough to bowl or bag (see Challah Notes). Cover; let rise for NO LONGER THAN 40 MINUTES.

4. Preheat oven to 425°F. Line 2 baking sheets with parchment paper, or grease 6 challah pans. Sprinkle liberally with cornmeal.

5. Divide dough into 6 equal portions. Working with one at a time, divide each portion into equal parts, depending on the number of strands you will braid. On a floured surface, form parts into long strands. Braid strands to form the challah shape. Repeat with remaining dough.

6. Place challos onto prepared sheets/pans. Brush with egg wash; sprinkle with oats. Brush with egg wash again, over the oats. This glazes the oats and helps them stick to the dough.

7. Bake for 15 minutes. Lower oven temperature to 375°F; bake for an additional 15-20 minutes or so, depending on size of challos. Remove challos from oven; place upside down on a towel to cool.

LIGHT AS AIR MARBLE CAKE

Two of my very close friends and I exchange funny anecdotes, daily struggles, and simple questions by group text. Also many recipes. This one is easy yet so impressive; whenever one of us bakes it we post a picture, with comments: "Look how high it came out this time," we write, or "I cannot get over how delicious this cake is," etc. My friend Debbie first introduced the recipe to us; she credited Karen Edelstein. It probably originated in someone's Bubbie's kitchen circa 1950's. It tastes that way. I've baked it almost every Friday since. The kids request it often. Nobody is bored of a classic.

Best part: I always have these ingredients handy ... no need to plan ahead.

I smile when I read Debbie's original introduction, clearly stating that this cake must be handled with the utmost care and respect. "Don't rush." "Beat the eggs long enough." "Use only dry utensils"... and so on. She's right; those precautions ensure you achieve the perfectly high cake you see pictured.

---

7 eggs, *separated*

2¼ cups sugar, *divided*

1 teaspoon vanilla sugar

1 cup oil

1 cup orange juice

2 cups flour

2 teaspoons baking powder

½ cup cocoa powder
(preferably Dutch process)

NOTE

To marbleize cake: At 5 to 6 different spots in the cake, dip a fork in and out of the batter in a swift motion, lifting some batter from the bottom. Use the fork to swirl it around a bit, mixing a bit more. This will give the cake a pretty marbleized effect.

TIP

Once cooled (after 3-4 hours), run a sharp knife around the perimeter of the cake and turn pan over. Cake should release from the sides of the pan. To transfer to a platter, run knife between the cake and the tube and the removable pan bottom.

1. Preheat oven to 350°F. In the dry bowl of a stand mixer fitted with the whisk attachment, on high speed, beat egg whites until foamy. Add 1 cup sugar, ¼ cup at a time, beating after each addition. Beat until stiff peaks form. Incorporate vanilla. Set aside.

2. In a second bowl, on medium speed, combine egg yolks, 1 cup sugar, oil, and orange juice. Reduce speed; slowly add flour and baking powder. Scrape down sides of bowl as necessary.

3. Using a metal spoon, gently fold egg yolk mixture into beaten egg whites, without deflating the batter, until no trace of white remains. Pour two-thirds of the batter into an ungreased, dry tube pan.

4. Return bowl with remaining batter to the mixer; add remaining ¼ cup sugar and cocoa powder. Mix until combined. Pour over the yolk batter; use a fork to marbleize the batters (see Note). Don't overdo it or a light chocolate cake will result.

5. Bake for 1 hour-1 hour and 10 min, or until a toothpick comes out with some moist crumbs attached. Remove cake from oven and immediately turn upside down (see Tip). Let cool.

LEMON CAKE

P || 1 10-INCH CAKE; 8-10 SERVINGS

Ask me what my favorite fruit is and I will reply, "lemon," in a heartbeat.

I buy lemons in bulk. Lemons add so much to any dish, whether you are baking or cooking, I find them indispensable. And no, the stuff in the bottle just won't do. Only fresh.

This lemon cake is a favorite in our house. We save it for special occasions ONLY. I like to prepare the cake part in advance and freeze it. The curd has to be prepared fresh, usually one day earlier. I use the same recipe for the lemon curd here as in the Deconstructed Lemon Meringue Pie (page 246). It's a great, fail-proof curd, and, best of all, I can prepare a double batch at one shot and use it for the cake and the dessert as well, resulting in two very different dishes. How's that for multitasking?

Thank you, Mrs. S., for sharing this recipe.

NOTE

Don't know what to do with the egg whites that you don't use in the Lemon Curd? Not to worry — egg whites freeze very well. You can defrost and use them in omelets or in any recipe calling for egg whites. Just remember to label how many whites are in the container.

FOR THE CAKE

6 eggs, *separated*

1½ cups sugar, *divided*

½ cup oil

¾ cup orange juice

2 cups flour

3 Tablespoons baking powder

pinch salt

1 Tablespoons lemon zest

FOR THE LEMON CURD

1¼ cups sugar

¼ cup cornstarch

¼ teaspoon salt

⅔ cup freshly squeezed lemon juice

5 Tablespoons margarine

1 egg, *at room temperature*

4 egg yolks, *at room temperature*

2 Tablespoons lemon zest

½ cup nondairy whipped topping

1. **Prepare the cake:** Preheat oven to 350°F. In the bowl of a stand mixer fitted with the whisk attachment, on high speed, beat egg whites with ¾ cup sugar until stiff peaks form. Set aside.

2. In a second bowl, on high speed, beat egg yolks with remaining sugar until thick and light in color. Reduce speed. Add oil and orange juice. Slowly add flour, baking powder, and salt. Carefully fold yolk mixture into beaten egg whites. Gently incorporate lemon zest.

3. Pour batter into an ungreased, dry tube pan. Bake for 55 minutes-1 hour, until a toothpick inserted into the cake comes out dry. Remove cake from oven and immediately turn upside down (see Tip, page 188). Let cool. Once cooled, use a sharp knife to cut the cake out of the pan. Cut the cake horizontally into 2 layers.

4. **Prepare the lemon curd:** Follow Steps 4 and 5 in the Deconstructed Lemon Meringue Pie (page 246).

5. After removing curd from the heat, wait 2-5 minutes for the curd to cool. Using the handle of a wooden spoon, press holes into the bottom cake layer. Pour half the curd over the bottom layer. Carefully top with second layer. Pour remaining curd over the cake, letting it drip decoratively down the sides. Store at room temperature in a cake dome; use within 3-4 days.

MRS. LIEBERMAN'S MIRACULOUS PESACH CHOCOLATE CAKE

Have you looked at this cake? Would you believe me if I told you it didn't have any flour, baking powder, or baking soda?

Pesach baking is a delicate matter. You don't want to be rushing this cake. Follow the instructions, give it its proper respect, and you will see great results. This is the only cake you will ever need, come Pesach. So rich and thick, it is a true crowd pleaser. I used to bake different tube cake variations each Pesach, but by now I know this one is everyone's favorite, and I just bake a few and call it a day.

TIP

A neat trick I recently learned: Once the cake is cool enough to handle, place the cake in its pan, upside down, into the freezer. Cut cake out of tube pan when frozen.

NOTE

A tube pan has a removable center with a tube, straight sides, and three spikes on top (see photo on page 189). Those spikes help the cake stand upside down to cool, so that it (hopefully) doesn't sink. Buy a light-colored pan without a nonstick coating. The cake will rise better.

9 eggs, *separated*

2 cups sugar, *divided*

pinch salt

¾ cup oil

1 heaping Tablespoon instant coffee granules dissolved in 1 Tablespoon water

½ cup cocoa

¾ cup potato starch

1. Preheat oven to 350°F.

2. In the bowl of a stand mixer fitted with the whisk attachment, beat the whites on high speed until foamy. Ever so slowly, add 1 cup of sugar. Beat until stiff peaks form. Set aside.

3. In a second bowl, beat eggs yolks and salt on high speed. Slowly add remaining cup of sugar, little by little. Beat on high until the yolks are a pale yellow.

4. Lower speed; slowly add oil and coffee.

5. Place cocoa and potato starch into a sifter. Ever so slowly and gently, incorporate the sifted mix into the egg yolk mixture. Keep stopping, sifting, mixing, stopping, sifting … little by little. Do not rush this. Scrape down sides as needed.

6. Fold chocolate mixture into the whites, mixing as gently as possible, until incorporated and no white is seen. Pour into an ungreased, dry tube pan; bake for 1 hour. (Do not use a nonstick tube pan! Only a metal one will do.)

7. Remove cake from oven; invert. Cool for at least 6 hours (better overnight) before cutting cake from pan (see Tip).

DOUBLE FUDGE MOUSSE CAKE

P || FF || GF || 1 (9 X 13-INCH) CAKE

Looking for something truly divine? Rich with chocolate but yet delicate? This is the type of cake that you'll label "broccoli quiche" when you freeze it, or it might never make it to Pesach.

You won't believe it's gluten free!

NOTE

The chocolate here is the star of the show. It is therefore imperative to use a good-quality baking chocolate with high cacao content (preferably 64% or above).

10 ounces baking chocolate, *divided*

½ cup oil

8 egg whites

⅔ cup sugar, *divided*

10 egg yolks

½ cup ground walnuts

½ cup ground filberts

1 cup shredded coconut

1. Preheat oven to 350°F. Grease a 9 x 13-inch baking pan.

2. In a small saucepan, over low heat, melt 8 ounces baking chocolate with the oil. Stir until combined. Remove from heat; let cool.

3. In the bowl of a stand mixer fitted with the whisk attachment, on high speed, beat whites until foamy. Reduce mixer speed; slowly add ⅓ cup sugar. Beat until stiff peaks form. Remove whites from bowl; set aside.

4. In the bowl of a stand mixer, combine yolks with remaining ⅓ cup sugar. Beat on high speed until light and creamy, about 3 minutes. Using a spatula, incorporate nuts, then fold in beaten egg whites. Fold in cooled chocolate.

5. Set 1 cup of batter into the refrigerator. Pour remaining batter into prepared pan. Bake for 50 minutes.

6. Spread shredded coconut on a cookie sheet; toast in the oven until just golden, about 5 minutes.

7. Once cake has cooled, melt remaining 2 ounces chocolate. Stir into reserved batter. Spread mixture over cake to glaze. Top with shredded coconut.

8. Keep cake refrigerated; it will stay fresh up to 4 days in the refrigerator.

THE BASIC CHEESECAKE

Confession:

Here we go (deep breath …).

When I follow a recipe, while baking or cooking, even my own recipe, I will do as follows: read. Ok. 2 teaspoons baking powder. Get the baking powder. Read again. 2 teaspoons. Get a measuring spoon. Read again. Measure 2 teaspoons. And so on …. You get the picture. Am I paranoid? Maybe. Not the only one to follow a recipe like this? Most certainly.

I'm really not sure why we do this. Maybe extreme fear of failure. Or short-term memory. Or trying to bake while chatting on the phone with your sister. Whatever the case, this recipe is probably the only one that I actually know by heart and I don't need to pull out my folder for it. That's because I've prepared it so many times already that it's part of me. OK. The short ingredient list helps as well.

NOTES

This cheesecake can be baked in store-bought graham cracker pie crusts as well. When doing that, I double the filling and divide the batter among 3 pie crusts.

Also, the sour cream topping can be replaced by the caramel sauce on page 201 if you prefer. Top with chocolate curls for a show-stopping presentation.

FOR THE CRUST

2 cups graham cracker crumbs

6 Tablespoons (¾ stick) melted butter

¼ cup chopped walnuts

FOR THE FILLING

2 (8-ounce) containers whipped cream cheese, *at room temperature*

¾ cup sugar

1 teaspoon vanilla sugar

3 eggs, *at room temperature*

FOR THE TOPPING

1 (16-ounce) container sour cream

2 Tablespoons sugar

1. Preheat oven to 350°F.

2. **Prepare the crust:** Mix together graham cracker crumbs, melted butter, and chopped walnuts. Press into a 9-inch springform pan. Bake for 10 minutes. Remove from oven and let cool.

3. **Meanwhile, prepare the filling:** In a stand mixer fitted with the whisk attachment, on medium speed, cream together the cream cheese and sugars. Add eggs, one at a time, beating after each addition. Beat until smooth. Pour batter into pan; bake for 1 hour, until center is mostly set.

4. Turn off oven. Let cool for about 10 minutes in the oven.

5. **Prepare the topping:** In a small bowl, use a fork to combine sour cream and sugar. Spread evenly over the cheesecake. Preheat oven to 350°F. Return cheesecake to oven; bake for 15 minutes. Let cool; refrigerate overnight before serving.

CHAVI'S EASY NO-BAKE CHEESECAKE

When my sister tells me something is divine, I know I'd better listen up. In her book, not many things are divine. A great balabusta, she takes pride in her cooking, and each one of her recipes is solid. So, that said, I wasn't surprised by this heavenly creamy cheese cake, which is not only delicious, but also no-bake and as easy as it gets.

It is always nice to get feedback after recipes have been published. I enjoy seeing what my readers liked (or didn't – constructive criticism is always welcome). The funniest email I ever received came after Ami printed this particular recipe. It was from three bachurim in a dira in Israel. They wrote, in humorous poetry form, that they had been craving homemade cheesecake for Shavuos but sans oven they were kind of stuck. And then they read about this no-bake cheesecake and decided to give it a try …. They loved it!

NOTE _____

I like to use the Scoop and Stack scoop by Cuispro to plate this cheesecake.

3 cups heavy cream

¾ cup sugar

2 (2.8-ounce) packages instant vanilla pudding (I use Osem)

2 (8-ounce) containers 95% Tnuva soft quark cheese

1 (8-ounce) container 91% Tnuva soft quark cheese

1 teaspoon instant coffee granules dissolved in 1 Tablespoon hot water

1 cup milk

1 (14-ounce package) tea biscuits (preferably a combination of vanilla and chocolate)

chocolate curls, *for garnish*

1. In the bowl of a stand mixer fitted with a whisk attachment, whip heavy cream on medium speed until mixture begins to thicken, about 30 seconds. Increase speed to high; whip until soft peaks form, 30-60 seconds, while adding the sugar slowly. Be careful not to over-whip.

2. Add instant pudding and cheeses. Mix on low to just combine. Finish by using a spatula to fold together. Set aside.

3. In a shallow bowl, combine coffee mixture and milk. One by one, dip each tea biscuit into the milk mixture, then place into a 9 x 13-inch pan, forming one row of darker cookies and one row of lighter ones if you are using vanilla and chocolate biscuits. Fill the entire bottom of the pan with cookies. You might have to cut the cookies in the corner a bit to fit well.

4. Spread a layer of cheese mixture (approximately one-third of the batter) over the cookies. Use an offset spatula to spread evenly. Repeat layering cookies and cheese mixture twice, ending with the cheese mixture. You will have 3 cookie layers and 3 cheese layers. Cover; refrigerate for at least 24 hours before serving.

5. To serve, slice into squares or rounds, as shown (see Note); garnish with chocolate curls.

CHOCOLATE CHEESE TRIFECTA

The first time I met this legendary cheesecake was at my eldest son's upsherin. My sister-in-law Zeldy had graciously offered to bake a cake; little did I know she'd walk in carrying the prettiest and most delicious cheesecake ever, which vanished in a matter of minutes. Needless to say, I immediately took her recipe and baked it for every possible occasion.

Fast forward five years. Walking into the annual shul get-together, I recognized a familiar-looking cheesecake with those beautiful layers. The three

shades were calling my name. One bite told me that it wasn't quite the same. This was lighter, creamier. Miri K. kindly revealed the secrets of this cherished family recipe, and after much tweaking and testing, I combined the two versions, taking the best features of both, melding them into one unique cheesecake.

This cake will be the center of attention at your Shavuos kiddush. Let its beauty adorn your Yom Tov table. Don't forget to taste it, too — it tends to just ... disappear.

FOR THE CRUST

- 1 (10-ounce) bag chocolate chip OR vanilla Ostreicher cookies
- ¼ cup (½ stick) butter, *melted*
- 2 Tablespoons brown sugar

FOR THE CHEESE BATTER

- 1 pound farmer's cheese, *softened*
- 2 (8-ounce) packages cream cheese (not whipped), *softened*
- 1 (16-ounce) container sour cream, *at room temperature*
- 1¾ cups sugar
- 2 Tablespoons vanilla sugar
- 6 eggs, *at room temperature*
- 6 ounces bittersweet baking chocolate
- 3.5 ounces good-quality milk chocolate
- 3.5 ounces good-quality white chocolate (I use Schmerling's Choco Blanc)

1. **Prepare the crust:** In the bowl of a food processor fitted with the "S" blade, pulse cookies until fine crumbs form. (Alternatively, you can crush them by hand. The vanilla ones are fairly easy to crush.) In a medium bowl, combine crushed cookies, butter, and brown sugar. Press into the bottom of a 10-inch round springform pan. Set aside.

2. **Prepare the cheese batter:** Place softened cheeses, sour cream, and sugars into a large mixing bowl. Using an immersion blender, blend the cheeses and sugars until creamy, for at least 4 minutes. This will be a bit challenging for the first minute, but will become easier as the cheeses blend. The blade of the blender helps break down all the little cheese particles, rendering a very silky cheesecake, so blend until no cheese particles are visible.

3. Add eggs, one at a time; blending each time until just combined.

4. Divide the batter equally into three bowls. Melt bittersweet baking chocolate (see page 171); add to one bowl. Stir gently until smooth; carefully pour chocolate batter into the pan, over the prepared crust, aiming for the center so that sides remain neat and even. Freeze cheesecake for at least 2 hours (this will guarantee nice, even layers).

5. While you wait, melt the milk chocolate. Add to the second bowl of batter; mix until smooth. Cover; refrigerate. Repeat with the white chocolate and third bowl of batter.

FOR THE CARAMEL

2 (3.5-ounce) bars white almond chocolate (I use Schmerling's), *chopped*

2 teaspoons corn syrup

2 Tablespoons prepared espresso OR prepared strong coffee

¼ nougat chips (I use Baker's Choice)

See full-size photo on following page.

6. Once the first layer is set, remove pan from freezer. Give the milk chocolate batter a quick stir; carefully pour it over the first layer. Return pan to freezer for 1½-2 hours. (This layer will freeze faster because cake is already cold).

7. Preheat oven to 350°F. Layer two sheets of heavy duty foil on the counter. Remove the cheesecake from the freezer; place it onto the foil. Fold the foil over the bottom of the pan tightly (to prevent water from the water bath from seeping into the cake).

8. Remove the white chocolate batter from the refrigerator. Give it a quick stir; gently pour over the milk chocolate layer.

9. Place springform pan into a larger pan. Fill larger pan halfway with hot water. Carefully place pan into the oven and bake for 1½ hours. (If at any point the cheesecake batter was frozen overnight, add 15 minutes to baking time.)

10. Turn off the oven. Remove cheesecake from water bath. Remove protective foil from around the cake. Return the cheesecake to the oven. Leave the door just a crack open and let cake cool slowly for 1½ hours. Cover; refrigerate overnight.

11. **Prepare the caramel:** In a small saucepan, over low heat, place white almond chocolate, corn syrup, and espresso. Melt chocolate, constantly stirring with a fork or a small whisk. After chocolate melts, add nougat chips; stir to combine. Remove from heat; let caramel cool for just a minute or two, while still stirring.

12. Uncover cheesecake. Using a paper towel, dab away any moisture that might have formed. Carefully pour caramel over cheesecake. Use an offset spatula to spread caramel evenly.

13. Run a knife around the edges of the cake; carefully release it from springform pan.

THE EUROPEAN CHEESECAKE

I knew I was getting somewhere when my sister-in-law walked in one day, looked at what I had in the fridge, opened her eyes wide, and whispered, "Kleinblatt's?"

No. I'm not giving you Kleinblatt's recipes. I wish. Using them for inspiration is as good as it gets, folks.

This cheesecake is European for mainly two reasons. It has a tart shell for a crust, and it uses

quark as opposed to the traditional American favorite, cream cheese. Quark, a form of soft cheese originating in central Europe, gives this cheesecake its characteristically dense but smooth texture.

*The credit for this recipe goes to my good friend from Switzerland, who came over to take a "quality control" bite and exclaimed, "Now **this** is cheesecake."*

FOR THE DOUGH

½ recipe Kaas Potjes dough
(page 208; see Note)

1 Tablespoon sugar

FOR THE CHEESE FILLING

4 eggs

1¼ cups sugar

1 teaspoon vanilla sugar

4 (8.8-ounce) containers
Tnuva's quark soft cheese
91% (or 95%)

¾ cup heavy cream

½ cup flour, *sifted*

¼ cup cornstarch

¼ teaspoon baking powder

juice and zest of 1 lemon

1 recipe Cream Cheese
Frosting, *facing page,
optional*

NOTE _____

The Kaaas Potjes dough is the one I use here. Halve the recipe or prepare the full amount and save the extra dough in the freezer for future use.

1. Prepare the dough according to directions. Refrigerate until well chilled.

2. Remove dough from refrigerator. Place dough between 2 floured pieces of parchment paper. Roll out into a circle, ¼-inch thick. Place dough into a springform pan, lining the bottom and sides. You can use any size or shape pan, 8-, 9- or 10-inch will all work fine. You will have enough dough and batter for any of those sizes.

3. Place pan into freezer for at least 30 minutes.

4. Preheat oven to 350°F. Remove pan from freezer. Line pan with foil; fill with pie weights, rice, or beans. Bake for 20 minutes. The dough will probably shrink a little bit, but don't fret, it's fine. Remove from oven; remove weights and foil. Sprinkle dough with 1 tablespoon sugar, making sure it covers the entire bottom surface. (The sugar will glaze over and form a protective barrier to keep the cheesecake base crisp and less soggy.) Return to oven for 8-10 minutes. Remove from oven; let cool a bit before adding the cheese filling.

5. **Prepare the cheese filling:** Preheat oven to 350°F. Position one rack in the center of the oven and one at the bottom.

6. In the bowl of a stand mixer fitted with the whisk attachment, on medium speed, combine eggs, sugars, and cheese until smooth and silky. Add heavy cream; beat for an additional minute.

7. Reduce mixer speed to low. Sift in flour, cornstarch, and baking powder, scraping down sides as needed. Stop mixing as soon as combined and smooth. Add lemon zest and juice. Mix for another second.

8. Fill a (9 x 13-inch) pan halfway with hot water. Place into oven on lower rack.

9. Add filling to prepared crust until it is three-quarters full. You might have some extra filling, depending on how big your pan is or how much your dough has shrunk. (If you have leftover dough, I recommend you prepare a smaller cake as well.) Place cheesecake pan on the middle oven rack. Bake for 1 hour 10 minutes. (Baking time is given for a 9-inch springform pan. Bake slightly less or more for an 8- or 10-inch pan, respectively.)

10. Turn oven off; open oven door just a crack. Let cheesecake rest in oven for an additional hour.

11. Remove from oven; let cool on counter until almost room temperature. Refrigerate overnight.

12. Remove from springform before frosting or ready to serve.

See full-size photo on previous page.

CREAM CHEESE FROSTING

This cheese cake is superb in its own right and does not necessarily need the cream cheese frosting. This was a creation that I came up with recently. It just doesn't happen every day that a photographer takes a picture of my cheesecake! We had to look super nice for the occasion.

1 (8-ounce) bar cream cheese, *not whipped, cold*

¼ cup butter, *softened*

1 cup sifted confectioners' sugar

½ teaspoon lemon juice

1. In the bowl of a stand mixer fitted with the paddle attachment, on medium speed, combine cream cheese and butter until smooth. Sift in confectioners' sugar and lemon juice.

2. Add frosting to a piping bag fitted with a star piping tip (Wilton's 1M). Creating the roses is much easier than it looks. When you pipe frosting on a cupcake, you pipe from the outer edges to the center. To make a rose, it's the opposite. You will start from the center and pipe around to the outer edges, moving your piping tip in a circle, twirling it around the middle. Keep looping until the rose is the desired width.

CANNONCINI
CREAM-FILLED PUFF PASTRY HORNS

You don't need much convincing to know that these are sublime. Just look at them: crunchy sweet dough filled with a light cream, combining the two into an exquisite bite.

Growing up, this was a special treat reserved for special occasions. They might look complicated to pull together, but don't get intimidated. They aren't. The horns can be prepared in advance and frozen (they are actually fun and not difficult to prepare). The cream stays fresh in the refrigerator. Even filled, these cannoncini can be stored for a day refrigerated.

FOR THE FILLING

1 cup heavy cream

4 ounces brick-style cream cheese, *at room temperature*

3 Tablespoons sugar

2 Tablespoons freshly squeezed lemon juice

FOR THE PASTRY HORNS

1 sheet puff pastry

sugar, *for sprinkling*

SPECIAL EQUIPMENT

cream horn molds

1. **Prepare the cream filling:** In the bowl of a stand mixer fitted with the whisk attachment, whip heavy cream on medium speed until mixture begins to thicken, about 30 seconds. Increase speed to high; whip until soft peaks form, 30-60 seconds. Transfer to a bowl; set aside. In the same mixer bowl, on medium speed, beat together cream cheese and sugar until soft and creamy. Add lemon juice. Use a spatula to fold in whipped cream. Refrigerate.

2. **Prepare the pastry horns:** Preheat oven to 400°F. Line a rimmed baking sheet with parchment paper.

3. Roll thawed puff pastry into a large rectangle. Using a pizza cutter, slice the dough lengthwise into ½-inch-wide strips. Working with one at a time, place the tip of a mold at the top of each strip. Wrap dough around the tip, overlapping dough slightly. Continue wrapping until the entire mold is covered. Brush the dough with a drop of water so that it seals well when wrapped. Cut off any extra length of dough; roll the mold gently, pressing it to seal the layers together. Repeat with remaining dough and horn molds.

4. Use a pastry brush to brush molded horns with water; sprinkle with sugar to give horns a nice sheen and crunch. Place on prepared baking sheet; bake for about 12 minutes, or until golden. Allow to cool. Slip the baked horns from the molds. Freeze horns until ready to serve.

5. To assemble, transfer refrigerated cream to a piping bag, preferably fitted with a small star tip. Pipe cream into horns. Serve immediately or refrigerate until ready to serve.

VIDEO TECHNIQUES

HOW TO WRAP DOUGH AROUND HORN MOLDS AND FILL BAKED HORNS WITH CREAM

WWW.ARTSCROLL.COM/OURTABLEVIDEOS

KAAS POTJES
(CHEESE POCKETS)

This one is, by far, my most requested recipe yet. Without fail, come every Erev Yom Tov, I will get a bunch of emails from random people who either misplaced the recipe or simply tasted it at a friend's house. I can almost say that I decided to write a cookbook only so that this particular recipe gets printed.

In my house, Kaas Potjes spell out Shavuos. And no matter how many batches I bake, there's never one left.

FOR THE DOUGH

14 ounces (3½ sticks) butter OR margarine, *softened*

4 eggs, *at room temperature*

2 egg yolks, *at room temperature*

1 cup sugar

6 cups flour

1 teaspoon baking powder

FOR THE FILLING

2 (8-ounce) packages cream cheese (not whipped), *softened*

5 Tablespoons (⅔ stick) butter, *softened*

⅔ cup sugar

2 teaspoons vanilla sugar

1 egg

1 egg yolk

2 teaspoons cornstarch

confectioners' sugar, *for dusting*

VIDEO TECHNIQUES

HOW TO ASSEMBLE CHEESE POCKETS, ADD FILLING AND GRATE DOUGH FOR THE TOPPING

WWW.ARTSCROLL.COM/OURTABLEVIDEOS

1. In the bowl of a stand mixer fitted with the dough hook, on medium speed, combine softened butter, eggs, and yolks; beat until butter is broken down a bit, about 2 minutes. Add sugar; continue to mix. Slowly add flour and baking powder. Mix until a nice, soft dough forms. (Dough might seem sticky, but that's OK, once it's chilled it will be more manageable.) Divide the dough into 3 parts. Place each part into a separate resealable plastic bag; refrigerate, preferably for a few hours or overnight.

2. **Prepare the filling:** In the bowl of a stand mixer fitted with the whisk attachment, combine all filling ingredients until creamy. Refrigerate until ready to use.

3. Preheat oven to 350°F. Prepare standard or mini muffin pans.

4. Using a box grater, grate one piece of well-chilled dough onto a plate. If the dough hasn't chilled enough, place it into the freezer for a bit. Refrigerate grated dough until ready to use.

5. Remove remaining dough from the fridge. Working with one piece at a time, roll out dough to ¼-inch thick. Cut rounds with a 3½-inch round cookie cutter or glass. Place rounds into a muffin tin, pushing down and pressing sides to cover all sides. Fill each with a heaping tablespoon of filling.

6. Place 1-2 tablespoons grated dough over each cheese pocket (be generous; this is what makes the pockets pretty), pressing down gently to attach them to the cheese filling.

7. Bake cheese pockets, 25-30 minutes, until golden. Let cool; dust with confectioners' sugar.

TASTY CHOCOLATE
CHEESE MUFFINS

Among my kid's favorite treats of all time, these muffins are simply delightful.

I also like to use this chocolate batter frequently (without the filling), sometimes to whip up a last-minute siyum treat (yes, my kids also show me that note after 9 p.m. the night before).

With no eggs in the batter, these are great chocolate cupcakes for anyone with egg allergy.

FOR THE CHEESE FILLING

2 eggs, *at room temperature*

1 cup sugar

2 (8-ounce) bars cream cheese (not whipped), *at room temperature*

FOR THE BATTER

3½ cups flour

¾ cup cocoa powder (preferably Dutch process)

2 teaspoons baking soda

2¼ cups sugar

1 teaspoon salt

1¼ cups whole milk

1 cup cold water

¾ cup oil

1 Tablespoon pure vanilla extract

5 teaspoons balsamic vinegar

FOR THE TOPPING

¾ cup chocolate chips

1 (3.5-ounce) bar white chocolate (I use Choco Blanc), *chopped into small bits*

PAREVE OPTION ____

To make pareve muffins, substitute the milk for water only and skip the cheese filling. This recipe doubles well too.

1. Preheat oven to 350°F. Line 2 muffin pans with paper liners.

2. **Prepare the cheese filling:** In the bowl of a stand mixer, on medium speed, beat together eggs, sugar, and cream cheese until smooth, about 2 minutes. Transfer filling to a piping bag fitted with a wide-rimmed piping tip. Set aside.

3. **Prepare the batter:** In the bowl of a stand mixer fitted with the whisk attachment, on low speed, stir together flour, cocoa powder, baking soda, sugar, and salt until evenly blended. Slowly add milk, water, oil, vanilla, and vinegar, stirring until the batter is smooth. Scrape down the sides as needed, mixing until well combined.

4. Transfer batter to a large resealable bag; snip off one corner. Pipe batter into prepared muffin tins, filling each cup half full. Then, press the cheese filling piping tip slightly into the batter; squeeze gently to pipe a generous squirt of filling into the batter. The chocolate batter will rise a bit as the filling goes in.

5. Sprinkle the top of each muffin with chocolate chips and chopped white chocolate.

6. Bake muffins until a toothpick inserted into the center of a muffin comes out clean, 26-28 minutes.

NOTE ____

Why is there vinegar in the muffin batter? Baking soda, the ingredient that makes these muffins rise, starts to work only when it comes in contact with an acidic ingredient. Some common types used in baking are lemon juice, buttermilk, and vinegar. Sweet balsamic vinegar, which has a flavor that goes well with the rich flavor of cocoa, is added to the batter here to give these muffins a deep, full flavor. Don't you worry, though, they won't taste anything like vinegar after the muffins are baked.

APPLE AND HONEY ROSH HASHANAH MUFFINS

D/P || FF || ABOUT 48 MUFFINS

At our house, Rosh Hashanah cannot happen without honey muffins. At least, that's the way my kids see it. It's a family project, and by now, a family tradition, too. This recipe was given to me by a relative in Israel who bakes them all the time and claims that no matter how many batches she bakes, there are never enough. She's absolutely right. We once baked a quadruple batch of these (sans the apples) for a bake sale on our block and we were left without a crumb!

NOTE

The apples are optional; I find that some children prefer the muffins plain. We add the apple for Rosh Hashanah (very loudly singing, "Dip the apple in the hooooneeeyy" as we do so) but throughout the year, we bake them plain.

TIP

I recently discovered an amazing gadget called "The Cupcake (or Muffin) Pen." It really removes the whole messy aspect of filling cupcake pans with batter. Look for it in specialty equipment stores.

FOR THE APPLES

2 Tablespoons butter OR margarine

4 Granny Smith apples, *diced*

4 Tablespoons sugar

1 teaspoon cinnamon

FOR THE MUFFINS

2 cups prepared tea, *lukewarm*

2 cups sugar

2 cups oil

2 cups honey

12 eggs

6 cups flour

2 Tablespoons baking powder

1 teaspoon baking soda

2 heaping Tablespoons cinnamon

1. Preheat oven to 350°F. Line a muffin pan with cupcake liners.

2. **Prepare the apples:** In a saucepan, melt butter over a medium-low flame. Add apples, sugar, and cinnamon; cook until apples are fragrant and soften a bit, about 15 minutes. Set aside to cool.

3. **Prepare the muffins:** In the bowl of a stand mixer, on medium speed, combine tea, sugar, oil, honey, and eggs. Mix until smooth. Reduce speed; gradually add flour, baking powder, baking soda, and cinnamon. Scrape down sides of bowl as needed.

4. Fill each muffin cup halfway with batter. (I like to use a cupcake pen for this; I find it very helpful.) Top with a teaspoon of prepared apples. Bake for 15-20 minutes, or until an inserted toothpick comes out almost dry with some moist crumbs attached.

212 · OUR TABLE

BUTTERY CHOCOLATE SCONES

The other day, I received a call from a relative. "We are stopping by to say hi! Don't prepare a thing. Just a coffee, maybe."

Right.

Three minutes later, I had scones in my oven. No, I'm not Mary Poppins. I just rely on my freezer for situations like these. I learned that from my mom: what to bake when, what to freeze, and how to have something ready when, in reality, you're anything but ready.

Ima never had the luxury of a kosher bakery just a few minutes away. We grew up with a constant stream of guests, visitors, tourists … and the occasional drifter. These guests were usually hungry, craving something other than the tuna sandwiches they'd been eating all week. Freshly baked cakes or cookies were the norm at my house. The fruit platter was constantly refilled. It seemed so easy, looking back, almost natural. Ima baked, and we munched. Until I had my own home, I didn't realize what it meant to never run out of something

good and fresh to serve. During a chat with an old school friend, this topic came up. She confided that she loved coming to my house after school because something delicious was always waiting. She said that my mother was usually in the kitchen, greeting us warmly, apron on and table set. Growing up, I hadn't noticed. I was sure that hot homemade rugelach were a standard. Hearing my friend talk about my home made me feel so good and a bit fuzzy inside. And I wondered: Will my children's friends remember our home so fondly?

Being a great hostess means being ready. Ready on time. Ready to receive people in a serene manner. Ready for unexpected visitors.

These scones are simply too wonderful to describe. I love the aroma that wafts around my house while they bake. Irresistible is an understatement. And since scones are only good the same day they are baked, I like to prepare and freeze them raw, only to bake as many as I need. It's the perfect pastry to serve next to coffee when you are having company: fresh, delicious, and oh so homemade.

---

8 Tablespoons plus 2 Tablespoons (1¼ sticks) frozen butter, *divided*

½ cup whole milk

½ cup sour cream

2 cups flour, plus more as needed

½ cup sugar, plus 1 Tablespoon, *divided*

2 teaspoons baking powder

¼ teaspoon baking soda

½ teaspoon salt

1 (3.5-ounce) bar 72% dark chocolate, *finely chopped*

1 (3.5-ounce) bar white chocolate (I use Choco Blanc), *finely chopped*

1. Line a baking sheet with parchment paper. Set aside.

2. Grate 8 tablespoons butter with a box grater. This will be easier if you hold the butter with a piece of parchment paper or plastic wrap. Place the grated butter into the freezer until ready to use (the colder the butter, the better).

3. Whisk together milk and sour cream. Refrigerate until needed.

4. In a medium bowl, whisk together flour, ½ cup sugar, baking powder, baking soda, and salt. Add grated frozen butter; toss with fingers until combined. Add milk mixture to flour mixture; fold together with spatula until just combined.

5. Use the spatula to transfer dough to a well-floured work surface. Sprinkle flour over the dough; knead until it just holds its

shape. Use more flour if needed. Dough will be crumbly, but that's normal. Try not to add too much flour or to overwork it. It just needs to hold together.

6. Roll dough into a rectangle, roughly 15 x 12 inches. Fold dough into thirds like a business letter (see photo, page 216, upper left), using a metal spatula to release dough if it sticks to work surface. Fold once again to form a small square. Transfer dough to a floured plate; chill in freezer for 5 minutes.

7. Remove dough from freezer; roll out into a square, approximately 12 x 12 inches. Sprinkle chopped chocolate all over the square and press down gently so that they are embedded in the dough (see photo, page 216, top right). Roll dough tightly to form a log (see photo, page 216, bottom left). Turn log seam-side down; press down to form a rectangle. Using a sharp knife, cut into 8 wedges (see photo, page 216, bottom right). Transfer to prepared baking sheet.

8. Melt remaining butter. Brush scones with melted butter; sprinkle with 1 tablespoon sugar. At this point you can bake the scones at 425°F for 20-25 minutes, until golden, or you can freeze them for later use. If frozen, bake at 375°F without prior defrosting, for 25-30 minutes, until golden.

9. Transfer scones to wire rack and let cool 10 minutes before serving.

See full-size photo on page 217.

BABKA SWIRLS

I was hoping that the FDA would come out with a statement saying margarine is healthier than oil. Oops, that didn't happen. Please don't start counting the sticks of margarine, I beg you (which is probably the first thing you'll do, right now, even before finishing the paragraph). (Yes, I know.)

Definitely don't email me about the quantity of margarine, either. (Babka is not a vegetable, a fruit, or a healthy choice of breakfast. It is what it is. Nobody said this was going to be healthy.)

I try not to use too much margarine either, but when it comes to babka, I go all out. If you are

going to have a piece of babka, have it all the way. The right way. With oozing chocolate, a crunchy bottom, soft dough, and incredible flavor. It doesn't get much better than this, in Babkaland.

This recipe was given to me by Nechy E. She likes to make large babkas with it. Feel free to do that; I just feel that there is more portion control with the swirls. With a whole babka, it was just too easy to take sliver after sliver, and before I knew it, the babka was history. So now I bake individual swirls and sometimes even manage to control myself after eating only three. No judging, please.

FOR THE DOUGH

2 ounces fresh yeast OR 3 Tablespoons dry yeast

1 cup plus 2 Tablespoons sugar, *divided*

1 cup warm water (110-115°F)

10 cups flour

1½ cups (3 sticks) margarine, *softened*

2 eggs, *at room temperature*

4 egg yolks, *at room temperature*

1½ cups nondairy coffee whitener

FOR THE STREUSEL

½ cup (1 stick) margarine, *softened*

1½ cups flour

1 cup sugar

1. **Prepare the dough:** In a small bowl, place the yeast, 2 tablespoons sugar, and warm water. Wait a few minutes for yeast to activate. Meanwhile, place the flour, remaining 1 cup sugar, margarine, and eggs into the bowl of a stand mixer fitted with the dough hook. Add coffee whitener and yeast mixture. Knead for a full 10 minutes, until dough is soft and elastic. Transfer to a bowl lined with a food-safe plastic bag. Cover; let rest for 1 hour.

2. Preheat oven to 350°F. Grease muffin pan cups with softened margarine, taking care not to miss any spots. (Try not to use the disposable pans. The Babka Swirls bake better in metal pans and the swirls will have straighter sides. Bake in batches if you don't have enough pans.)

3. **Prepare the streusel:** In a bowl, combine streusel ingredients, mixing with your fingers until crumbs form. Store in refrigerator until ready to use.

4. **Prepare the filling:** Combine cocoa and sugars in a small bowl. Set aside.

5. After dough has risen, divide into 6 equal parts. Working with one part at a time, using a rolling pin, roll into a square. Try to roll it as thin as possible without ripping holes. Generously smear the square with approximately ½ stick of softened margarine. Sprinkle

FOR THE FILLING

1 cup Dutch processed cocoa powder

2 cups sugar

⅔ cup confectioners' sugar

½ cup vanilla sugar

1½ cups (3 sticks) margarine, *divided*

1 egg, *lightly beaten, for egg wash*

chocolate filling over margarine, covering evenly and not skimping. Roll up one side of the square, jelly-roll style. Using a sharp knife, slice into swirls about ¾-inch thick. Place into prepared muffin pan cups. Repeat with remaining dough. (If preparing traditional babkas, instead of slicing the rolled dough into individual buns, simply fold each roll in half and then twist 3 times. Transfer to large parchment paper-lined loaf pans.) Brush with egg wash; immediately sprinkle with prepared streusel. Cover with a towel; let rise 20-30 minutes.

6. Bake Babka Swirls for 25-35 minutes. Pop them out of the muffin pans while still hot, otherwise oozing chocolate will cool and harden, rendering them almost impossible to remove from pan. (Large babkas will need to bake for 45-60 minutes, until nicely browned.)

See full-size photo on following page.

IRRESISTIBLE CHOCOLATE PECAN BARS

These bars aren't baked too often at my house. If they are baked, I kinda hide them in the washing machine or something. They are just impossible to resist. Therefore, I only bake them for special occasions or when someone really insists. Don't say I didn't warn you.

For this recipe I like to use a Pyrex pan (either 1 [9 x 13-inch] or 2 [11-cup] pans). No, I don't especially enjoy washing dishes, the reason I even own a few of those is because I firmly believe that for some specific recipes the Pyrex enhances the taste and texture. Otherwise it's disposable pans all the way. So, yes, the crust here just needs Pyrex. And I love the fact that my pan comes with a cover. Although it's a shame Pyrex doesn't make covers with a lock.

Thank you, Tari M., for sharing this unique recipe with us.

FOR THE CRUST
1½ cups flour
½ cup (1 stick) margarine, *softened*
½ cup crushed salted pretzels
¼ cup brown sugar

FOR THE FILLING
3 eggs
¾ cup corn syrup
¾ cup sugar
2 Tablespoons margarine, *melted and cooled*
1 teaspoon pure vanilla extract
1½ cups chocolate chips
3½ cups pecans

1. Preheat oven 350°F.

2. **Prepare the crust:** In the bowl of a stand mixer, or by hand, combine all crust ingredients; mix until just crumbly. Evenly spread the crumb mixture into the Pyrex pan; use a spoon to press down and compact the crumbs. Bake, uncovered, for 15 minutes. Remove from oven; let cool a bit while you prepare the filling.

3. **Prepare the filling:** In the same bowl (no need to wash), combine eggs, corn syrup, sugar, margarine, and vanilla. Whisk until combined. Add chocolate chips and pecans; mix with a fork until just combined. Gently pour over cooled crust.

4. Bake for 35-40 minutes, until sides are set and center is still a bit bubbly. Let cool; slice into bars. Store in an airtight container at room temperature.

CHOCOLATE CHIP SQUARES

Kids are the ultimate judges. They are brutally honest. They don't consider the fact that you stayed up till 2 a.m. the night before, baking that cookie they unceremoniously dropped into the trash.

That said, let me assure you that these squares are always a crowd pleaser, and are happily eaten and even requested again and again, especially by children.

NOTE

Bake in ramekins and serve warm, with a scoop of homemade ice cream, for a delectable Yom Tov dessert.

1½ cups oil

6 eggs

1½ cups sugar

2 cups brown sugar

2 teaspoons vanilla sugar

2 cups potato starch

1½ cups ground almonds

1 (10-ounce) bag chocolate chips

1. Preheat oven to 350°F. Line two (9 x 13-inch) pans with parchment paper. Set aside.

2. In the bowl of a stand mixer fitted with the paddle attachment, on medium speed, combine oil, eggs, and sugars. Gradually add potato starch and almonds.

3. Divide batter equally between the prepared pans. Sprinkle evenly with chocolate chips.

4. Bake for 40-50 minutes, until a toothpick comes out dry when inserted. Allow to cool; then cut into 1½ x 1½-inch squares.

5. Place in an airtight container with sheets of parchment paper between layers; squares will stay fresh for up to a week. This recipe doubles well and freezes nicely.

OUTRAGEOUS CHOCOLATE CHIP COOKIES

This recipe comes with history attached. I know, I know, I have a story to each recipe. But for me, food is always linked to some memory or place, hence the always-present-attached-story. This particular memory takes me back to Newark airport, about a week post-9/11, when I was trying to get onto a flight. There was no telling if anybody had a chance; all you could do was wait and see. And wait we did. My dear mother-in-law made sure to provide all the nutrition a gal might need in this situation (read: massive bag of freshly baked chocolate chip cookies). I pulled it out of my carry-on bag while waiting on line, wondering why I had agreed to take along such an exorbitant number of cookies. Let's just say that by the time the flight was ready for boarding, I had an empty bag and many new friends.

These cookies have been a staple at our home for over a decade now. Yell at me all you want (Margarine?! Nooooo!), but for a crispy outside and chewy inside, you need margarine, and nothing else will do.

We Mullers bake these at every opportunity: a Yom Tov, after a taanis, or a birthday party — these cookies will be there, and we never tire of them.

1 cup (2 sticks) margarine, *softened*

½ cup sugar

½ cup brown sugar

½ cup brownulated sugar

1 teaspoon pure vanilla extract

2 eggs

1 teaspoon salt

1 teaspoon baking soda

2¼ cups flour

2 cups chocolate chips

1 (15-ounce) bar bittersweet baking chocolate (I use Shufra), *chopped*

½ cup chopped walnuts

1. Preheat oven to 350°F. Line two baking sheets with parchment paper. Set aside.

2. In the bowl of a stand mixer fitted with the paddle attachment, on medium speed, cream margarine and sugars until light and fluffy. Reduce mixer speed; slowly add vanilla and eggs, one at the time.

3. Slowly incorporate salt, baking soda, and flour. Add chocolate chips, chopped chocolate, and walnuts; mix until just incorporated.

4. Using a medium sized ice cream scoop, scoop about 8 balls of dough per sheet. Leave about 1½ inches between them, as they will spread.

5. Bake 9-13 minutes, depending on if you prefer your cookie chewy or crispy. For a chewier cookie, bake for the shorter time, for a crispier cookie, bake longer.

6. Using a spatula, transfer cookies to a cooling rack to cool.

TIP FOR FREEZING COOKIE DOUGH

These cookies are great to have in the freezer, baked or raw. I save the center cores of paper towels for the raw dough. Roll dough into a log on a sheet of parchment paper. Roll the dough into the paper, twist the ends, and slide it into the paper towel cylinder for a neat way to freeze the cookie dough log. Label them clearly, right on the cardboard! To bake, slice into rounds and place on a parchment-lined baking sheet. Alternatively, freeze scoops of dough on a tray. Place frozen dough balls into a resealable bag. Then, just remove and bake as many as you need. Frozen cookie dough will need a few additional minutes of baking time.

BROWNIE BRITTLE

I still remember standing in Costco and holding a bag of brittle with real longing. It looked so, so good. But it wasn't chalav Yisrael. I had a hard time putting it back on the shelf.

I found myself craving it for the rest of the day too. Until a little voice told me, "Ma, why don't you try to make some yourself?" Why had I not thought of that?! Sometimes we need a 5-year-old to tell us what to do. So out came my favorite brownie recipe. And on went the oven.

The rest is delicious, crunchy, satisfying history.

2 cups sugar

2 teaspoons vanilla sugar

1½ cups flour

¾ cup cocoa

½ teaspoon baking powder

1⅓ cups oil

4 eggs

2 Tablespoons corn syrup

about 1 cup broken salted pretzels OR other topping, *such as nuts, chocolate chips, etc., optional*

1. Preheat oven to 350°F. Line two baking sheets with parchment paper.

2. In the bowl of a stand mixer fitted with the whisk attachment, on low speed, combine sugars, flour, cocoa, and baking powder. Add oil, eggs, and corn syrup. Mix until just combined, scraping down the sides as needed.

3. Divide the batter between the two baking sheets; using an offset spatula, spread into an even layer. Scatter broken pretzels over the batter. Bake for 35-40 minutes. Let cool completely; then break into pieces. Store in an airtight container or freeze until ready to serve.

NOTE

The outer edges will be more crunchy and the center more cakey. In my house, this works well because I prefer the really hard pieces while my kids like the center ones. If you prefer everything to be crispier, I recommend baking the brittle as two long strips on the baking sheet (as opposed to filling the entire pan). Also, you can skip the topping completely; this brittle is delicious as is.

DAIRY OPTION

Use 2 (3.5-ounce) bars white almond chocolate, chopped, for the topping (I use Schmerling's).

See full-size photo on following page.

FUDGE BOMBS

We (entire household, neighbors, family, friends, and whoever was available to taste) couldn't come up with an appropriate name for these incredible cookies, no matter how hard we tried. What do you name something that's crispy and delicate on the outside but chewy and fudgy on the inside? Oh, and let's not forget the chocolate. Lots of chocolate.

"Fudge Bombs" seemed appropriate. Get ready for a real indulgence.

These cookies are gluten free, perfect for Pesach, yet we bake them year round — they are that good.

NOTE

It is imperative that you measure the egg whites. Eggs vary in size, especially from country to country, and in this particular recipe, the egg whites are key.

See full-size photo on following page.

3 cups confectioners' sugar

1 Tablespoon vanilla sugar

⅔ cup cocoa powder

⅛ teaspoon salt

½ cup egg whites, *divided (from approx. 3 eggs, but you must measure!)*

1½ cups chocolate chips OR 2 (3.5-ounce) bars good-quality pareve chocolate (I use Schmerling's 72%), *chopped into small pieces*

1. Preheat oven to 350°F. Line two baking sheets with parchment paper.

2. In a bowl, whisk together the sugars, cocoa, and salt. Add two-thirds (about 5 tablespoons) of the egg whites. Stir. Add remaining egg whites; mix until combined. Batter should be thick and glossy.

3. Stir in chocolate chips.

4. Drop spoonfuls of batter onto prepared sheets, about 5 cookies per sheet. Leave plenty of room between cookies as they spread while baking.

5. Bake for 12-14 minutes, until the tops look lightly cracked.

6. Let cookies cool completely on baking sheet. Do not move them. When cooled, transfer to an airtight container; store for up to 3 days. Cookies freeze well.

THIN, DARK, AND CHEWY COOKIES

D/P || FF || ABOUT 4 DOZEN COOKIES, DEPENDING ON SIZE

These cookies became notorious once published in Ami. (Notorious, I learned, is not a good way of being famous). People almost lost a knuckle while grating the chocolate needed for this recipe.

That said, I reluctantly put this recipe on the back burner. I really like these cookies. The buttery flavor melded so well with the chocolate. Crunchy but chewy. So incredibly delicious. I couldn't understand why spending 20 minutes grating chocolate by hand could make someone so miserable that they would stop grating, wash their chocolaty hands, and sit down to write me a "colorful" email.

Fast forward 4 years, and this last Pesach, with recipes for my cookbook in my mind, I got a recipe for a cake with chocolate shavings in it. Which you grate in the food processor. Ta da! It worked! Now I knew how to salvage this cookie and have it come back to where it deserves to be: in the cookbook.

See full-size photo on previous page.

3 (3.5-ounce) bars 55% bittersweet chocolate (I use Schmerling's Noblesse)

1 cup (2 sticks) butter OR margarine, *softened*

1½ cups packed brown sugar

1¼ cups sugar

2 eggs

1 Tablespoon pure vanilla extract

1½ cups flour

½ cup cocoa

1¼ teaspoons baking soda

1 Tablespoon salt

8 ounces (2 cups) finely diced walnuts

1 (3.5-ounce) bar white chocolate, *optional*

1. Using a food processor fitted with the coarse shredding blade (aka the kugel blade), process the chocolate until it is shaved; set aside.

2. In the bowl of a stand mixer fitted with the paddle attachment, on medium speed, cream butter with the sugars until light and fluffy, about 2 minutes.

3. Add eggs, 1 at a time. Add vanilla. Reduce speed; gradually add flour, cocoa, baking soda, and salt, being careful not to overmix. Add walnuts and shaved chocolate. Mix until just combined.

4. Chill dough for at least 20 minutes in the refrigerator. Preheat oven to 325°F. Line a baking sheet with parchment paper.

5. Using a large ice cream scoop, scoop balls onto prepared baking sheet (you will only fit about 5 cookies on the sheet). Spray a flat (pareve) meat pounder (or the bottom of a glass bottle) with cooking spray. Press cookies down gently to flatten them. Alternatively, you can use the palm of your hand.

6. Bake for 15-17 minutes. The cookies should be firm but still a little soft. They will continue to harden while cooling.

NOTE

I'm a big fan of butter, always have been, always will be. These cookies have always been *milchig* at our house, until I came up with the Mint & Chocolate Hot Cookie Dessert (page 264). I must say they are really good when they're pareve too. It's your call.

JUST RIGHT COOKIES

Salty and sweet get together here for a memorable cookie that will have you craving more. We call them "Just Right" because they truly are.

Restrain yourself from eating the raw cookie dough.

NOTE

If you don't use nuts, you may want to add more granola (any type will do), snacks, or chocolate to compensate.

1½ cups flour

1 teaspoon baking powder

½ teaspoon baking soda

1 teaspoon salt

7 ounces (1¾ sticks) butter OR margarine, *at room temperature*

1 cup granulated sugar

½ cup light brown sugar

1 egg

1 teaspoon pure vanilla extract

1 cup granola, *store-bought*

½ cup crushed salted pretzels

1 cup chocolate chips OR 1 (3.5-ounce) bar good-quality dark chocolate, *chopped*

½ cup chopped pecans OR other nuts, *optional*

1. Preheat oven to 375°F. Line 2 large baking sheets with parchment paper. Set aside.

2. In medium bowl, whisk together flour, baking powder, baking soda, and salt.

3. In the bowl of a stand mixer, beat butter and sugars at medium-low speed until just combined, about 20 seconds. Increase speed to medium; beat until light and fluffy, about 1 minute. Using a rubber spatula, scrape down bowl. Add egg and vanilla; beat on medium-low until fully incorporated, about 30 seconds. Scrape down bowl again.

4. Add flour mixture; mix until just incorporated and smooth. Gradually add granola, pretzels, chocolate, and nuts, mixing until well incorporated, ensuring that no flour pockets remain and ingredients are evenly distributed.

5. Scoop dough into balls, each about 1½ tablespoons; roll between palms to shape balls. Place balls on prepared baking sheets, spacing them about 2½ inches apart, 8-12 per sheet. Freeze at least 20 minutes, or refrigerate at least one hour before baking. (They will still spread very much.)

6. Bake one sheet at a time until cookies are deep golden brown, 13-16 minutes, rotating baking sheet halfway through. Using a spatula, transfer cookies to cooling rack to cool.

See full-size photo on previous page.

NINA'S BISCUITS

These biscuits do not need any embellishments. What they do need is a tall glass of milk.

2 cups potato starch

1 cup sugar

1 Tablespoon vanilla sugar

1 cup ground almonds

¾ cup ground coconut

2 eggs

1 cup oil

1. Preheat oven to 350°F. Line a baking sheet with parchment paper. Set aside.

2. In a bowl, whisk together potato starch, sugars, nuts, and coconut. Add eggs and oil, mixing until just combined.

3. Shape dough into ¾-inch balls. Place onto baking sheet about 1½ inches apart.

4. Bake for 16-18 minutes, until golden but still light. Cool biscuits on wire rack.

5. Store biscuits in an airtight container for up to a week.

ALMOND CHEWS

Every writer needs that humbling moment when a recipe is published with a mistake. I say "needs," and I mean it. Until that very moment, I didn't realize how many people around the globe were actually taking the time, spending the money on ingredients, and trusting me with my recipes. This recipe, compliments of my sister Esti, was printed in my second article with Ami, in their Pesach supplement. I made a mistake in the amount of almonds needed ... and let me tell you, I learned about checking and rechecking recipes the hard way. I was mortified. So many people had tried these cookies, because they looked soooo good, and because I urged them to do so, telling them they had never tasted anything better. Which was all true. But I missed one small detail.

Ever since that day, I check each recipe once, twice, three times, always remembering that awful mistake.

But back to these cookies. They are fantastic. I mean it! And I checked the recipe 7 times over.

6 egg whites
2¼ cups sugar
4 (6-ounce) bags ground almonds

1 Tablespoon fresh lemon juice
1 (3.5-ounce) bar good quality pareve chocolate

1. Line two cookie sheets with parchment paper. Set aside.

2. In a bowl, beat egg whites until stiff peaks form. Gradually add sugar, ¼ cup at a time, until stiff and glossy.

3. Add ground almonds and lemon juice; mix until just combined.

4. Chill dough in refrigerator for 1 hour.

5. Preheat oven to 350°F. Using a mini ice cream scoop (1½ inches in diameter) scoop out the batter, drop it into your hand, roll into a ball, drop onto prepared baking sheet, and press down with a damp hand. You can place cookies close together; they will not expand much.

6. Bake for 12-13 minutes. Cookies will seem raw but harden a bit as they cool. You want to make sure not to overbake so as not to lose the chewy texture. A good way to tell if the cookie is ready is by lifting it after it has cooled a bit. The bottom should be golden.

7. While cookies cool, melt chocolate in a double boiler or microwave (see page 171 for information on melting chocolate).

8. Dip Almond Chews halfway into melted chocolate. Replace on baking sheet; place in the refrigerator for a few minutes to set. The cookies are delicious plain too, even if you don't dip in chocolate.

9. Store in an airtight container for up to 5 days.

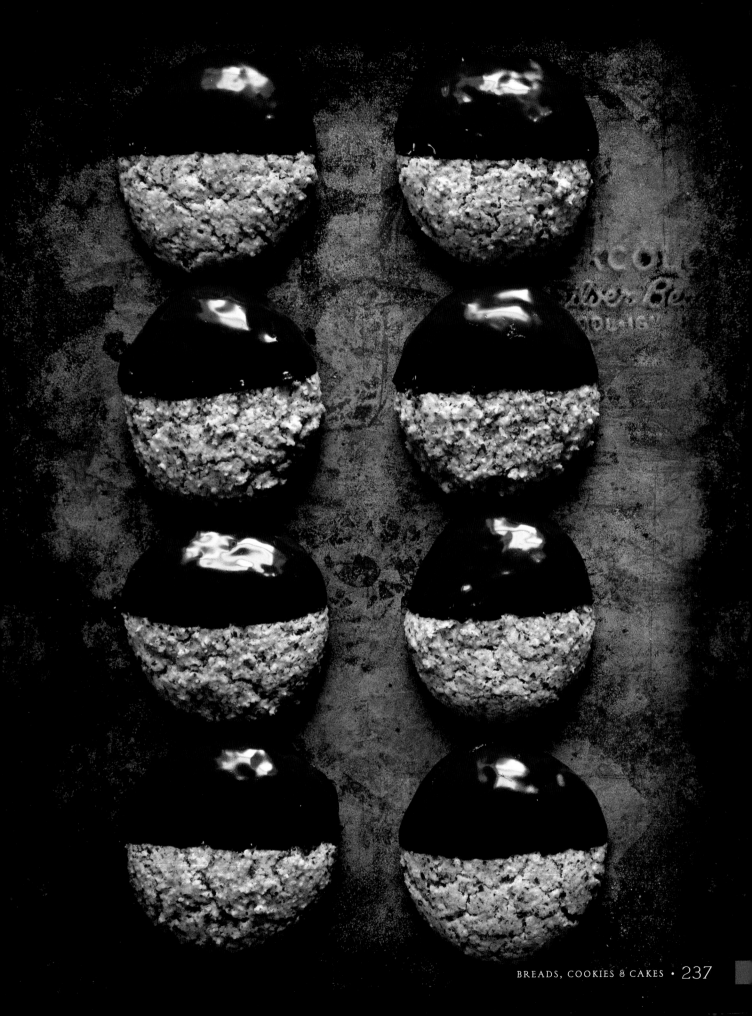

DAIRY CHOCOLATE CHUNK COOKIES

I'm very lucky to have a daughter as first child. I got to the stage where I can say, "We need some cookies in this jar" (I'm very subtle with my hints, I know), and cookies magically appear. But I recently started thinking twice before dropping said hints. Reason being that said Child A loves to whip up these particularly rich and delicious Dairy (!!) Chocolate Chunk Cookies. Her reasoning? They are quick. No mixer needed. Always loved. Sooooooooo good, like ridiculouuuuus (or whatever exclamation is currently hip with teenagers).

She happens to be one hundred percent right. I guess I will have just one more and then diet tomorrow.

16 ounces good-quality baking chocolate, *chopped*

⅔ cup butter

⅔ cup flour

½ teaspoon baking powder

½ teaspoon salt

2 cups sugar

4 eggs, *at room temperature*

2 cups chocolate chips

1 (3.5-ounce) bar white chocolate (I use Choco Blanc), *chopped into small pieces*

1. In a medium bowl, combine chopped chocolate and butter. Melt in the microwave, stopping from time to time to mix, until smooth. Alternatively, melt in a small saucepan over low heat. Let cool a bit; set aside.

2. Place flour, baking powder, and salt into a sifter. Set aside. Add sugar and eggs to a large bowl. Using a whisk, mix until well blended. Add the cooled melted chocolate; stir until blended.

3. Sift in flour mixture, a little at a time, stirring after every addition.

4. Stir in the chocolate chips and chopped white chocolate. Refrigerate batter for at least 1 hour.

5. Preheat oven to 350°F. Line two baking sheets with parchment paper.

6. Using a spoon, scoop up a small amount of cookie dough, roll into a ball, and place onto prepared baking sheet. Press down with the palm of your hand to flatten a bit. Repeat with the remaining batter; bake until the sides are firm and the centers are soft to the touch, about 15 minutes. Do not overbake or the cookies will be dry. Transfer cookies to a cooling rack to set completely.

DESSERTS

OUR CELEBRATIONS

Do you remember your birthdays? The ones when you turned 8, 7, maybe even 6? I do.

I remember my mother staying up late, waiting for a cake to cool enough so it could be frosted. I remember my sisters helping me wrap the pekalech for my friends. I remember wearing my favorite Shabbos dress and insisting on a specific hairstyle.

I think of all this, and more, as I pull myself out of bed while everyone is still asleep.

In truth, all I want is a few more minutes under the covers. But I know, just as every mother knows, these wee morning hours are the only ones I can steal in my already full day.

The house is quiet and dark. The counters are clean. I'm grateful I pushed myself to straighten up last night. I turn on the coffee machine, and while I wait, I start my morning prayers. With my siddur in my hand, I think of my mother. I always knew she was up and about when I smelled freshly brewed coffee and heard the radio playing.

My machine is out of coffee; I reach for a new bag. These little rituals, like opening a new bag of coffee, give me joy. I never tire of that. I stick my nose into the bag and inhale deeply. I miss my mom; but there's no time to waste. My daughter is turning 13 and I have invited all her friends for a Shabbos sleepover. Crazy, I know. I must whip up her favorite dessert and hide it before she wakes, or she will know something is up. She always knows what menu I'm cooking, partially because we plan it together, mostly because she helps with every step.

Deconstructed Lemon Meringue Pie is her ultimate favorite. It is usually reserved for Yom Tov. I'm hoping her friends will like it too.

She's too old for a classic streamers-cake-hats-and-gifts type of party; I figure a special dessert is the way to go.

The egg whites are beating loudly in the mixer. I add the first ¼ cup of sugar and pray no one is wakened by the noise. I think back to my fifth birthday. I remember schlepping to kindergarten the banana cookies I helped my mother bake. I had dipped all the ends into the melted chocolate. I was so proud of my work.

Will my children remember the cakes I baked for them before the sun came up? Will they look

back as fondly? I know they will. And that is why I push myself to give them these memories. This is my children's childhood. And it's up to me to make it memorable.

Piping meringues is so therapeutic, I find. The slow and steady motion so rewarding. I have time to think now, with a clear head, before my day begins. I think of everything that needs to be accomplished today and write it down, between tasks. The list is long but I am energized and confident it can be done.

Child B makes his first appearance in the kitchen. He is wearing the white shirt I prepared for him last night. Of course. Rosh Chodesh. I almost forgot! He plugs in the waffle maker while I put the butter into the microwave to melt. Rosh Chodesh means waffles. Or pancakes. Either way, an occasion to celebrate.

For a moment he stares at the freshly piped meringues, wondering, and then gives me an adorably knowing smile. We don't need to say a word. He knows Child A all too well, and he is happy for her, even though he seriously dislikes Lemon Meringue Pie, whether constructed or deconstructed.

Come May, it will without doubt be Mint & Chocolate Hot Cookies for him.

MOMMY'S APPLE COBBLER

P || FF || 2 COBBLERS OR
8-10 INDIVIDUAL RAMEKINS

I'm really not sure how to explain this but I firmly believe that this is the ultimate cobbler. Ever. The best you've ever tasted. The aroma alone, of the apples cooking with the cinnamon, is so enticing. On many occasions, at family simchahs and such, Mommy has whipped up a batch just to "make everyone feel at home, with that wonderful smell."

This apple cobbler is so perfect that we must have it every Shabbos. I am still trying to figure out why it is so good and what makes it so much better than your typical cobbler. It's still a mystery. All I know is that it is quick and easy, freezer friendly, and everyone likes it. To me, that's enough.

NOTE

I usually prepare this apple cobbler in advance and freeze it before baking. When I need one, I just remove it from the freezer and bake it for a little longer than the recipe instructs. Another great trick is to double the crumb mix and freeze the excess in a resealable plastic bag. This way, I only need to slice a few apples and I'm all set to make a fresh cobbler.

8 Granny Smith apples (do not substitute)

¼ cup orange juice

¼ cup sugar

about 2 teaspoons cinnamon, *to taste*

1 cup brown sugar

1½ cups white whole wheat OR regular flour

½ cup (1 stick) margarine

1. Preheat oven to 350°F.

2. Peel, core, and slice apples. In a bowl, combine apples with orange juice, sugar, and cinnamon. Divide apples between 2 pie pans or 8-10 ramekins. (Any oven-to-table dish will work as well.)

3. Place brown sugar, flour, and margarine into a second bowl. Using your fingers, combine them, forming a crumb (some of the crumbs should be pea-sized). Scatter crumbs over apples.

4. Bake, uncovered, for 45-50 minutes, depending on size of your dish. Cobbler is ready when edges begin to caramelize and crumb is becoming brown. Store at room temperature; serve, preferably, warm.

DECONSTRUCTED LEMON MERINGUE PIE

I loooove lemon meringue pie. No, that is actually not so true. I love the **idea** of lemon meringue pie. You know, tart lemon curd, sweet meringue … it all sounds so perfectly right until I dip my fork into that gooey meringue that actually tastes a bit like sea foam. I never understood why it's acceptable to serve practically raw egg whites (a few minutes in the oven ain't cutting it) on a cake. I'm not saying this from a "don't eat raw eggs" point of view. (Hey, I'm the one who puts raw eggs in my Caesar dressing.) No, that doesn't bother me. I just think the mound of egg whites on the pie looks good, but tastes offensive.

So, that is why I started experimenting. At first I tried baking the pie longer (didn't work, the curd was dry and ruined). Then came baking the meringue separately (messy to eat; didn't look right). Next, I decided to bake the meringues separately, crush them, and serve them with a lighter lemon curd. With lots of berries, let's not forget. And … success! No, it's not lemon meringue pie, it's more of a pavlova. But, to me, it's perfection.

The meringue recipe is actually Victoria Dwek's. Blush. (Yes, I asked; she let me print it.) It's amazing how different a meringue can be while using the same few ingredients. I'd been trying different recipes for a while and then I met Victoria. And her amazing meringues that just melt in your mouth like a cloud. Sheer genius.

There won't be a Yom Tov without this dessert and I am perfectly OK with that.

FOR THE LEMON CURD

1¼ cups sugar

¼ cup cornstarch

¼ teaspoon salt

⅔ cup freshly squeezed lemon juice

5 Tablespoons margarine

1 egg, *at room temperature*

4 yolks (reserved from the meringues), *at room temperature*

2 Tablespoons lemon zest

½ cup nondairy whipped topping

VIDEO TECHNIQUES

HOW TO MAKE LEMON CURD AND MERINGUES, SEED POMEGRANATES AND ASSEMBLE DESSERT

WWW.ARTSCROLL.COM/OURTABLEVIDEOS

1. **Prepare the lemon curd:** In a medium-sized saucepan, combine sugar, cornstarch, and salt. Whisk to combine. Add lemon juice and margarine; place pan over medium heat. Once margarine has melted, bring to a simmer, whisking constantly. Make sure no lumps are left.

2. Place egg and yolks into a small bowl. Beat with a fork until combined. Remove about ¼ cup of lemon mixture from the pot and add to the eggs. Mix vigorously and quickly to prevent curdling. Add egg mixture to the pot; stir together, whisking constantly, over low heat. After 3-5 minutes, you will notice the curd thickening. Make sure curd does not reach a boil; keep at only a low simmer. Once curd has thickened, stir in the lemon zest; remove from heat.

3. Transfer curd to a bowl; cover with plastic wrap. Press plastic down gently so it adheres to the entire surface. This will prevent a thick crust from developing. Let cool at room temperature for 2 hours.

4. In the bowl of a stand mixer fitted with the whisk attachment, whip the nondairy whipped topping until stiff peaks form. Using a spatula, fold together with the lemon curd, starting with about ½

FLOURLESS MOUSSE CAKE

P || FF || GF || 8 SERVINGS

Flourless, maybe. But flavorless? No way. This dessert is always a crowd pleaser. The kind that makes your Pesach guests wonder if you are serving chometz.

Thank you, Mrs. Lieberman, for sharing this delicious recipe with us.

8 ounces good quality pareve chocolate (I use Schmerling's Noblesse)

1 Tablespoon instant coffee granules

8 eggs, *separated*

⅔ cup sugar

⅛ teaspoon salt

1. Preheat oven to 350°F. Line a 9-inch round pan with parchment paper.

2. Using a double boiler (or microwave) melt the chocolate until smooth, stirring from time to time. Add coffee; stir to combine. Set aside.

3. In the bowl of a stand mixer fitted with the whisk attachment, on high speed, beat egg yolks until thick, gradually adding sugar. Continue beating on high speed for a full 5 minutes, until mixture is pale yellow and thick. Reduce speed; add melted chocolate, beating until just incorporated.

4. In a second bowl, on high speed, beat egg whites with salt to stiff peaks. Using a spatula, fold chocolate mixture into whites, gently mixing until combined well and no streaks of white are visible. Remove 4 cups of batter; refrigerate. Pour remaining batter into prepared pan.

5. Bake for 25 minutes. Turn off oven; let stand in oven for 5 minutes. Remove from oven; let cool. Cake will settle and fall a bit, but that's expected. Once cake is completely cooled, spread with reserved 4 cups batter. Freeze until ready to serve.

6. Cut into wedges while frozen; let thaw about 10 minutes before serving, so that the mousse is nice and creamy.

EXOTIC FRUIT SALAD

My kids are obsessed with passion fruit. They'll pick a passion fruit over a bag of sour sticks any day of the week. It's great, I know, but it's the kind of healthy choice that will make me broke at $2.99 a pop.

I believe this fascination started on a trip to England, years back. I'm not sure why, but passion fruits in London are pretty common and inexpensive. As a result, every time I traveled to London, or, as a matter of fact, every time anyone I knew did, I'd make sure we'd shlep back at least a dozen passion fruits. My sister who lives there knows this is her only ticket into our home.

This fruit salad needs only 2 passion fruits to give it that "pop" of flavor. But if you cannot find them, don't fret. It will be delicious even without it.

½ pineapple, *diced*

½ cantaloupe, *diced*

2 mangos, *diced*

4 persimmons, *diced*

2 Granny Smith apples, *not peeled, diced*

6-8 kiwis, *diced*

3 pomegranates, *seeded*

2 passion fruits

orange juice, *to cover*

1. For a beautiful presentation, as shown in the photo, spend a few minutes dicing the fruits with care. You want small, even cubes.

2. Combine all diced fruit in a bowl; add pomegranate seeds. Scoop pulp and seeds from the passion fruits; add to bowl. Add orange juice to cover entirely. Transfer to a lidded container to store in the refrigerator if not using immediately. Fruit salad is best served the same day, but will stay fresh for two days, refrigerated.

NOTE

When it comes to preparing a fruit salad, there are no set rules. A salad that's prepared in August will not and cannot be the same as the one prepared in January. Therefore, trust yourself and create your very own combination. I give you here a selection of fruits (the ones I used for the picture), but you can change it all to your liking. The secret lies in the orange juice. Covering the fruit with juice ensures that the fruit will stay juicy and crisp.

WÄHE — SWISS FRUIT TART

I grew up staring at these fruit tarts. Notice I wrote "staring" as opposed to "eating." No, I wasn't on a diet quite yet; I just grew up in Lugano, Switzerland, a beautiful town with (almost) no kosher stores. Lugano is renowned for its pasticcerie – little boutique-like pastry shops – where every tart or brioche is displayed in the window like jewelry and, once purchased, wrapped up like a gift. Fancy is an understatement.

Some pasticcerie needed reservations and proper attire. You could just imagine us, drooling at those displays every morning on our way to school.

My favorite was always the Wähe, so shiny, crisp, and inviting. Throughout the years I perfected my recipe, little by little, and although I cannot taste the authentic one, I'm pretty sure I got it right. While testing this recipe, I baked dozens of tarts and had my sisters come over to taste and approve. It was so wonderful to watch their eyes light up once they recognized this childhood treat! We all dug in and, for a moment, we were kids again, back in Lugano ....

---

1 sheet puff pastry

¼ cup ground almonds OR ground walnuts

fruit of your choice (apples, peaches, apricots, plums, rhubarb, fresh or frozen), *not peeled, sliced very thinly*

⅓ cup soy milk

1 egg

1 Tablespoon cornstarch

¼ cup apricot jam, *divided*

confectioners' sugar, *for dusting, optional*

NOTE

This tart has become my go-to recipe for last-minute surprise guests. Always a pleasure, always tasty, it takes very little time to cook and assemble.

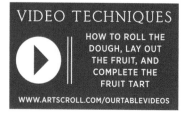

VIDEO TECHNIQUES

HOW TO ROLL THE DOUGH, LAY OUT THE FRUIT, AND COMPLETE THE FRUIT TART

WWW.ARTSCROLL.COM/OURTABLEVIDEOS

1. Preheat oven to 400°F. On a piece of parchment paper, roll out the puff pastry into a rectangle. I recommend using the Silpat mat.

2. Using a sharp knife, being careful not to cut all the way through, score a frame along the perimeter, about 1-inch from the edge. The incision will help keep the fruit and custard in its place; it will puff up as a frame while baking.

3. Carefully lift half of the rectangle, fold over, and sprinkle the parchment paper underneath with half the ground nuts (see top left photo on facing page). Carefully replace dough over nuts; repeat with other side. Sprinkle remaining nuts inside the frame (the nuts will help keep the dough crisp).

4. Arrange fruit neatly inside frame (see top right photo on facing page), creating pretty patterns. (You can freeze tart at this point.) Place tart with its parchment paper onto a rimmed baking sheet. Bake for 10 minutes.

5. Meanwhile, combine soy milk, egg, cornstarch, and 2 tablespoons jam in a measuring cup or bowl with a spout. Whisk vigorously until combined and all lumps are almost gone. (I like to strain this mixture, but it's not a must.) Remove puff pastry from oven and pour liquid very carefully over the tart. You might not need all of it, depending on how much fruit you used.

6. Return tart to oven for an additional 15 minutes.

7. Once the tart has cooled a bit, heat the remaining apricot jam in a small saucepan, until it starts to bubble on the sides. Using a pastry brush, brush hot jam over the entire surface, very carefully. This will give the fruit that glossy, professional look (see lower photo below; you can see that the two left columns of fruit have not yet been glazed). Store at room temperature or in the refrigerator, covered with a clean cotton kitchen towel. Serve with a dusting of confectioners' sugar (optional).

See full-size photo on following page.

POTS DE CRÈME

A twist on the typical version, these pots de crème are salty and sweet, infused with irresistible salted caramel. A real indulgence. And better yet, one that can be prepared in advance.

NOTE

This dessert is very rich. A little bit goes a long way; therefore, I like to serve them in small espresso cups.

2 cups heavy cream

½ cup milk

½ teaspoon pure vanilla extract

½ teaspoon sea salt, *plus more for sprinkling*

1 cup sugar

2 ounces baking chocolate (I use Shufra), *finely chopped*

6 egg yolks

1. Preheat the oven to 325°F. Heat heavy cream, milk, vanilla, and salt in a small saucepan over medium heat until mixture just starts to bubble. Remove from heat; cover to keep warm.

2. In a medium pot, combine sugar and ¼ cup water over medium heat. Stir until sugar dissolves. Continue cooking but don't stir any longer. Just swirl the pan from time to time. Cook until sugar is amber in color, about 10 minutes. Remove from heat; carefully add warm cream mixture. The mixture will bubble violently. Add chopped chocolate; stir until smooth.

3. In a medium bowl, whisk egg yolks (by hand) until combined. Add about one-third of the caramel sauce, whisking constantly; then add the remaining caramel. Whisk until smooth. Strain through a fine sieve and pour into a large measuring cup.

4. Pour the mixture into 8 ramekins or about 14 espresso cups. Set those into a baking dish; add enough hot water to the dish to come about halfway up the sides of the ramekins. Cover the pan tightly with foil; bake for 50 minutes.

5. Remove the ramekins from the water; let cool at room temperature. Cover ramekins with plastic wrap and refrigerate until cold, preferably overnight. Sprinkle with sea salt before serving. Pots de crème can be prepared 3-4 days in advance. Keep refrigerated.

INDEX

SOURCES

Set Your Table, *Lakewood, NJ and Monsey, NY.* 732.987.5569
pages 17, 19, 39, 41, 57, 74, 75, 199, 265

Verdini Petit Greens, *Lakewood, NJ.* 732.364.1133
pages 19, 21, 34, 85, 89, 115, 121

Photo Credit: Morris Antebi, page 141

MALKY'S OLD-FASHIONED APPLE BAKE

P || FF || GF ||
2 (9 X 13-INCH) PANS

There's this recipe in my mother-in-law's handwritten and stained cookbook entitled, "Malky's Apple Bake." I never thought much about it while preparing it year after year, sometimes a few times in a row, come Pesach. I never once wondered who Malky was. Then, one day, my mother-in-law told me about this incredible woman who was a good friend, an amazing mother, and a true saint. She unfortunately passed away young, leaving small children behind. And that's how I found out that I actually not only knew Malky's daughter, I was even friendly with her. My son and her son are good friends. I immediately gave her this recipe, knowing she would appreciate baking a dish her mother had baked, too.

9 Granny Smith apples, *peeled and sliced*

cinnamon, *to taste, optional*

4 eggs, *separated*

1½ cups sugar, *divided*

½ cup oil

½ cup potato starch

½ cup orange juice

1 cup ground walnuts

1 cup chopped walnuts

1. Preheat oven to 350°F. Divide apples between two 9 x 13-inch pans. Sprinkle with cinnamon, if using.

2. In the bowl of a stand mixer fitted with the whisk attachment, beat egg whites on high speed until foamy. Slowly add ½ cup sugar; continue beating until stiff peaks form. Set aside.

3. In a second bowl, beat yolks with ½ cup sugar, oil, potato starch, and orange juice. The mixture will be runny. Fold into the whites, mixing until uniformly blended. Pour over the apples in the two pans.

4. In a small bowl, combine walnuts and remaining ½ cup sugar. Sprinkle over apples in each pan. Bake for 1 hour-1 hour and 20 minutes, depending how crispy you like the top.

NOTE

This apple bake freezes well. Bake it for 1 hour. When ready to use, return frozen apple bake to oven to warm up before serving, allowing it to re-crisp.

My mother-in-law prepares this apple bake countless times over the course of Pesach. She loves this recipe in particular because it yields two pans, one to be enjoyed immediately, one to freeze for a later use. Little does she know, but the second pan doesn't always make it to the freezer ... yup, it's *that* good. And it has apples in it. So we all convince ourselves we are eating light (you know, taking a break from the Fudge Bombs, p. 229) and polish off one pan after the next. Sigh.

REFRESHING CITRUS FRUIT SORBET

P || FF || GF || 10 SERVINGS

This sorbet is so deliciously genuine and refreshing. After a late summer meal, nothing hits the spot better than some homemade sorbet. See the Note for a grapefruit variation.

NOTE

Serve scoops of sorbet over diced fruit for a nice presentation.

To prepare the grapefruit version: Substitute 5 cups grapefruit juice for the orange juice and the lemon juice.

2 cups water

1½ cups sugar

4 cups orange juice

1 cup freshly squeezed lemon juice

1. In a saucepan, over low heat, combine water and sugar. Stir until sugar is dissolved. Add juices; stir to combine. Divide between two (9 x 13-inch) aluminum pans (use only aluminum; otherwise it won't freeze as well). Freeze overnight.

2. Remove pans from freezer and break mixture into a few pieces. Working in batches, place pieces into a food processor that has been fitted with the "S" blade. Pulse until ice turns into a soft sorbet.

3. Use an ice cream scoop to scoop it out into neat balls. Place prepared scoops onto a baking pan; freeze. Scoops are ready to serve when frozen.

MINT & CHOCOLATE HOT COOKIE DESSERT

All chocolate and mint combination lovers: beware. You will get hooked. This luscious dessert has just the right balance of intense chocolate flavor and fresh mint. The cookie is best served warm (keep on the blech on Shabbos), topped with ice cream and warm fudge sauce. I think I will skip the meal and head straight to dessert.

NOTE _____

If serving on Shabbos or Yom Tov: Layer cookies in a 9 x 13-inch pan and keep on hot plate, in a warm, not-too-hot area. Do the same for the fudge sauce. Fudge sauce might char if kept over high heat too long. To serve, see Step 5.

FOR THE ICE CREAM

6 eggs, *separated*

⅓ cup sugar

1 teaspoon vanilla sugar

4 Tablespoons Dutch processed cocoa

1 (8-ounce) container nondairy whipped topping

½ (7-ounce) box chocolate mint thins, *chopped into small squares*

FOR THE COOKIES

1 batch Thin, Dark, and Chewy Cookies (page 232)

FOR THE FUDGE SAUCE

6 ounces good-quality chocolate, *chopped*

½ cup (1 stick) margarine

1 teaspoon water

1 teaspoon Dutch processed cocoa

1 teaspoon sugar

1 Tablespoon corn syrup

1. **Prepare the ice cream:** In the bowl of a stand mixer fitted with the whisk attachment, beat egg whites with sugars until stiff peaks form. Reduce speed to low; slowly add the cocoa, egg yolks, and nondairy whipped topping. Mixture will thin considerably.

2. Pour mixture into a deep loaf pan (I use an aluminum pan; the ice cream freezes faster, lessening the chance of the ice cream separating). Sprinkle with mint thins; swirl around a bit. Freeze.

3. Bake cookies as directed in recipe. Set aside.

4. **Prepare the fudge sauce:** Combine chocolate and margarine in a double boiler set over a pan of simmering water, or melt in the microwave in 30-second increments. Stir until smooth; stir in water, cocoa, sugar, and corn syrup. Fudge can be prepared in advance and rewarmed briefly before using. I love this fudge because it hardens as soon as it touches the cold ice cream, forming a shell.

5. To serve, place one warm cookie on each plate; top with a scoop of ice cream and a generous drizzle of fudge sauce.